D0409788

CAR
SCIENCE

Dorling Kindersley

DK

LONDON, NEW YORK,
MELBOURNE, MUNICH, and DELHI

Senior editor Ben Morgan
Editors Wendy Horobin, Deborah Lock, Alexander Cox
Senior designers Claire Patane, Karen Hood
Designers Laura Roberts, Sadie Thomas, Hedi Gutt
Illustrators Chris Longhurst, Alex Bec, Richard Burgess
Production controller Pip Tinsley
Production editor Siu Chan
Jacket designers Karen Hood, Natalie Godwin
Jacket editor Mariza O'Keeffe
Design manager Rachael Foster
Publishing manager Bridget Giles
Creative director Jane Bull
Publisher Mary Ling

Consultants Dr Jon Woodcock, Chris Woodford, Chris Longhurst

First published in Great Britain in 2008 by
Dorling Kindersley Limited,
80 Strand, London, WC2R 0RL

Copyright © 2008 Dorling Kindersley Limited
A Penguin Company

2 4 6 8 10 9 7 5 3 1
SD285 – 05/08

All rights reserved. No part of this publication may be reproduced, stored
in a retrieval system, or transmitted in any form or by any means, electronic,
mechanical, photocopying, recording, or otherwise, without the prior written
permission of the copyright owner.

A CIP catalogue record for this book is available from the British Library

ISBN: 978-1-40533-200-2

Colour reproduction by Alta Image, London
Printed and bound by Leo Paper Products, China

Discover more at
www.dk.com

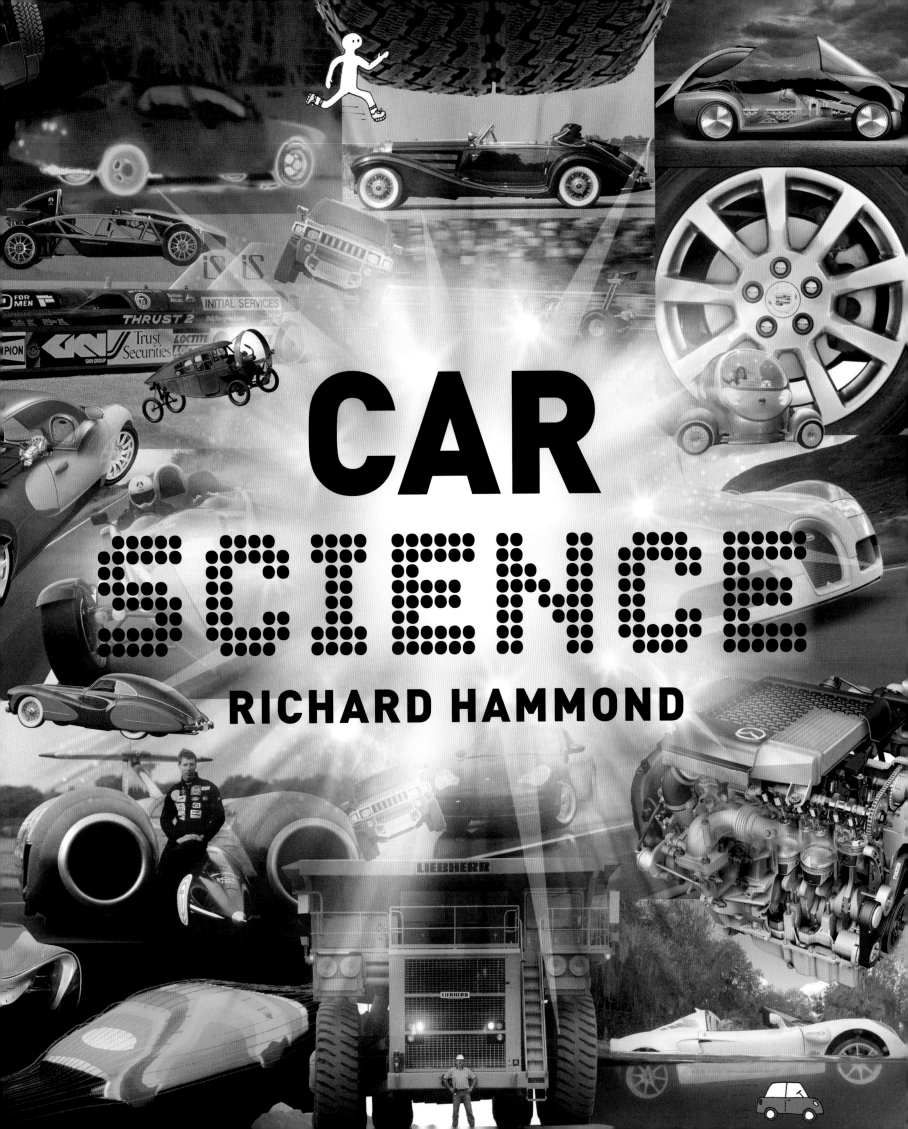

CAR SCIENCE

RICHARD HAMMOND

THRUST 2

INITIAL SERVICES

Trust Securities

LIEBHERR

Contents

1 Power

2 Speed

3 Handling

4 Technology

Introduction

Cars are crammed full of science. How fast they go, how quickly they can stop and how furiously they can go around a corner is all to do with science. And that's a good thing because two things that I really love are cars and science. How convenient, two of my favourite things all in one.

I know people who can tell the difference between a 1985 and 1986 Ford Fiesta from 500 metres in a snowstorm and who can remember the part number for a 1965 Morris Minor handbrake cable, but what they can't explain to me is the difference between power and torque.

Things like this are very useful for us to know. Lewis Hamilton and his mates in Formula One don't just drive their cars faster and faster until they crash and then remember to go a little bit slower next time; they understand what makes their cars stick to the road like an octopus wearing velcro shoes on a carpet. And because they understand the science involved they can help their engineers make the cars go even faster and therefore win races and become rich and famous.

Lots of people driving on the road don't really understand the science in their cars. If they did they wouldn't drive so close to the car in front on the motorway because

they'd know about things like inertia and momentum, and would know that if the car in front stops dead they'll not be able to stop in time. And if they knew a lot about the science of cars they'd know that stopping suddenly from 70 mph (113 km/h) involves a lot of forces. And tears and bruises.

It's a huge subject so we've been very sensible and split this book into four chapters: Power, Speed, Handling, and Technology. Each chapter covers everything you need to know to be a real motoring boffin. How a turbocharger works, how petrol is made; we'll look inside gearboxes and learn why a Formula One car's brakes glow yellow when it's stopping. And at the end we'll look at the sort of cars that we might be driving in the future.

Throughout the book we'll be meeting one of the world's first boffins, Sir Isaac Newton (you can't miss him, he's an old-looking bloke with crazy dress sense and a massive wig). Most of us know that one day an apple fell on Isaac's head and he realised that gravity existed, but he came up with loads of other brainy ideas and theories, too; most of which are very important to cars.

We know you'll learn a lot, we hope you enjoy doing so.

Power is one of the most exciting words in the English language. Politicians love it and so do car enthusiasts because it makes our cars go fast. And driving a fast car is much more fun than sitting in the Houses of Parliament arguing about the price of eggs.

So where does power come from? It's all to do with converting energy from one form (fuel) into another (movement). It's really quite simple, as you're about to find out.

Some people are never satisfied with what they've got and want even more, so we'll look at ways of making more of what we call "horsepower". Like making engines bigger, or making a small engine more powerful by cramming more fuel into it.

Incidentally, why on Earth is it called horsepower ...

Power

Goodbye horse!

The history of the car is really the history of **FUEL.** Ever since people invented the *wheel*, they've tried powering vehicles with everything from donkeys to chip fat. For a long time, *horse power* was the best option. The first true motor cars didn't appear until the invention of the **PETROL** engine.

Muscle power

Stone Age motoring 10,000 BC

In the beginning, muscle power was the only way of travelling or carrying stuff about on land. Heavy objects had to be dragged, which was back-breaking work, even if you used a few logs to make the going easier. It was a long, long time before wheels were invented, around 4000 BC in what's now Iraq. It wasn't simply a matter of chopping logs into round slices – someone also had to invent the tricky axles that go through the middle. There was one handy alternative to muscle power: water. Wherever there were rivers, people could use them as roads by travelling on rafts, canoes, or other types of boats – the oldest form of transport in the world.

Horse power

Horse-drawn carriage

Around 4000 BC, the fearsome warriors of Mongolia tamed wild horses and then rode into neighbouring countries on murderous raids. The horse soon caught on everywhere, and it wasn't long before someone put horses and wheels together and came up with horse-drawn carts and carriages. Animal power remained the only form of transport on land for more than 5000 years.

Coal power

During the 1700s, inventors in England discovered how to harness the energy in coal to make vehicles move, doing away with the need for horses. These "steam engines" used a coal fire to boil water and make steam, which then drove pistons to push the wheels round. But all the water, coal, and steel made the vehicles much too heavy to run on normal ground, so they had to roll along steel rails – and so trains were invented. Steam trains were great for hauling huge loads, but small personal cars remained no more than a dream.

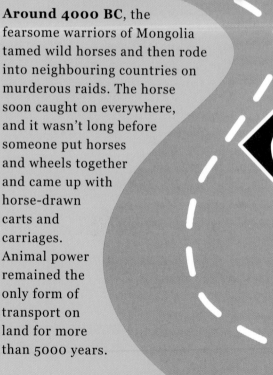

Steam engine, 1808

Solar power

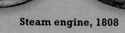

In one way or another, all cars are powered by second-hand solar energy. So why not simply use the Sun's energy directly? The answer is that the energy in raw sunshine just isn't sufficiently concentrated. In contrast, fuels like petrol contain huge amounts of second-hand solar energy concentrated into a small space. Nevertheless, some engineers

Harnessing the sun

What do all the different power sources on these pages have in common? Believe it or not, all of them supply energy that came originally from the Sun. Nearly all the energy we use on Earth comes from the Sun, and it usually comes to us via plants. Petrol, diesel, and coal are called "fossil fuels" because they come from fossilized plants.

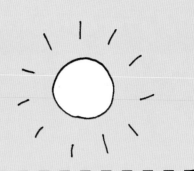

Battery power

In the late 1800s there was a race to invent the "horseless carriage" – a small, lightweight vehicle that didn't need rails. Coal was too heavy to use for fuel, so people tried other things, including gas, gunpowder, and something we now think of as modern: batteries. For a while, batteries seemed to be the answer – by 1897 New York had a fleet of electric taxis, and in 1899 the world land-speed record of 68 mph (109 km/h) was set in an electric car. But the batteries were heavy and cumbersome relative to the power they supplied, and they burned out if you tried to go fast.

Petrol power

The real breakthrough in the race to create the horseless carriage came when a German inventor, Nikolaus Otto, stole an ingenious idea from a French rival, Joseph Lenoir – and then improved it. Lenoir had built an "internal combustion engine", so named because it burned fuel inside a metal engine rather than on an open fire. Lenoir's engine used gas, but in 1876 Otto adapted it to burn petrol. It worked brilliantly – and so began the age of cars. Soon petrol cars built by the likes of Henry Ford in the USA were all over the world.

Henry Ford in
Model N Ford, 1905

The future...

So what's next? Petrol and diesel, which have been the motoring world's favourite sources of power for a century, could be on the way out, and the next big fuel might be hydrogen. Hydrogen is a clean fuel because it doesn't directly cause pollution: the only waste product it makes is water. And a clever device called a fuel cell can use hydrogen to make electricity, which can then be used to drive the wheels of electric cars. But there are a few snags to iron out before hydrogen takes over: like finding ways of making it, storing it, and delivering it to cars.

Electric car, 1896

Ford Focus

Honda FCX Clarity
fuel-cell car

powered by large solar panels that produce only a trickle of electricity. To make the most of their weak power, the cars are ultra-streamlined and lightweight, with room for only one person who has to lie down. And they aren't very fast.

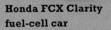

ENERGY

You might think that the way cars work has nothing in common with the human body, but you'd be very wrong. When it comes to the way cars and bodies use **ENERGY**, they do just the same job (but don't put spaghetti in your car).

Human body

The chemical wizardry that frees energy from food inside our bodies produces heat. Heat is invisible to the human eye, but with a special camera we can photograph it. This thermogram of an ice skater shows her body is much warmer than her chilly surroundings. The bare skin of her face is losing heat especially fast.

Spot the difference:

1 A **body** gets energy from **food** molecules. These are made of long chains of carbon atoms joined together by plants. The Sun's energy became trapped in the molecules as the plants constructed them.

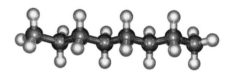

Spaghetti

2 Inside a **body**, **food** molecules react with oxygen sucked in from the air. The reaction breaks down the bonds between carbon atoms and rearranges the atoms into new combinations. This frees the trapped energy. Oxygen and carbon atoms join to make carbon dioxide, which the **lungs** must breathe out.

3 The chemical energy freed from **food** molecules is converted into new forms of energy: heat and movement.

Cars and bodies are powered by the same basic equation:

 FUEL + OXYGEN →

The energy that powers bodies and cars originally comes from the Sun as light energy. Plants convert light into chemical energy, which then becomes trapped when dead plants are turned into food or petrol. The chemical energy is then changed into kinetic energy (movement energy) by a car's engine or a human body. Energy never really gets "used up" – it just keeps getting changed from one form to another.

Light energy → **Chemical energy** → **Chemical energy again** → **Kinetic energy**

 # Car

A **car** gets energy from **fuel** molecules. These are made of long chains of carbon atoms joined together by plants. The Sun's energy became trapped in the molecules as the plants constructed them.

Petrol

Inside a **car**, **fuel** molecules react with oxygen sucked in from the air. The reaction breaks down the bonds between carbon atoms and rearranges the atoms into new combinations. This frees the trapped energy. Oxygen and carbon atoms join to make carbon dioxide, which the **exhaust** must breathe out.

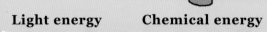

The chemical energy freed from **fuel** molecules is converted into new forms of energy: heat and movement.

The thermogram of a car shows heat leaking out of the engine bay. Car engines harness the explosive power of heat to drive their moving parts.

ENERGY +  CO$_2$ + WATER

What makes it GO?......

If someone asks you to explain in three words how a car works, here's what to say ... ☞

Of course, there are some differences between cars and bikes – cars can't do very good wheelies, for instance. But when you look at the parts of a car that actually make the wheels go round, it all turns out to be surprisingly similar to your average push-bike. Let's take a closer look...

... like a bike!

Pump action

On your BIKE ...

When you ride a bike, you power it by pumping your feet up and down vertically. The pedals are connected to the bike by levers called cranks, which turn the up-and-down motion into *rotation*, which is the kind of motion wheels need. The rotation gets fed to the wheels through the chain and gears. So: your legs go up and down, the wheels go round and round. That pushes you forward.

Gear

Crank

Pedal

The pistons in the engine pump up and down separately, but they're all joined together at the crankshaft. At the end of the crankshaft is a heavy metal wheel – a flywheel – that smooths the motion. The flywheel also helps keep things moving thanks to something called *inertia*. We'll find out a lot more about that later in the book.

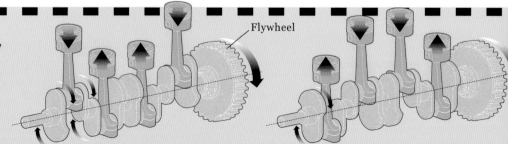

Flywheel

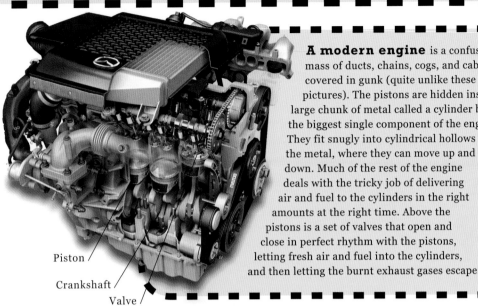

A modern engine is a confusing mass of ducts, chains, cogs, and cables, all covered in gunk (quite unlike these shiny pictures). The pistons are hidden inside a large chunk of metal called a cylinder block – the biggest single component of the engine. They fit snugly into cylindrical hollows in the metal, where they can move up and down. Much of the rest of the engine deals with the tricky job of delivering air and fuel to the cylinders in the right amounts at the right time. Above the pistons is a set of valves that open and close in perfect rhythm with the pistons, letting fresh air and fuel into the cylinders, and then letting the burnt exhaust gases escape.

Piston

Crankshaft

Valve

... and in your CAR

Now for the car engine. Deep inside it, hidden underneath the confusing mass of bits and pieces, is a row of metal cylinders called pistons that pump up and down, just like your feet on a bike. The pistons are joined to levers called cranks, which turn the up-and-down motion into rotation. As with a bike, the rotation is then fed to the wheels through the car's gears.

4 The driveshaft turns round the **wheel axle** (via a few more cogs), and the wheel axle turns the wheels. Job done.

3 The crankshaft turns round **gears** (cogs) in the **gearbox**. Then the gears turn round a metal bar called a **driveshaft**.

1 **Pistons** pump up and down like legs.

Gearbox

2 **Cranks** (levers) connected to the pistons turn the up-and-down motion into rotation, turning round something called the **crankshaft**.

The powerful motion of the engine has to get to the wheels. It's passed along a chain of different parts like a relay race, with all these parts spinning round powerfully. Together, these parts of a car make up what's called the **powertrain**.

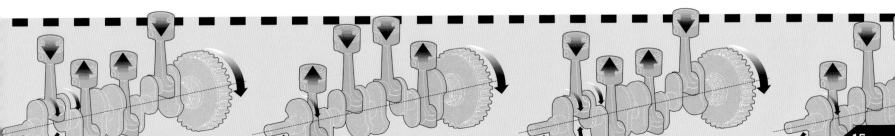

Fire power
The science of combustion

Combustion / *noun*
1: an act of burning.
2: a chemical reaction (oxidation) that makes heat and light.

As we've just seen, the pistons in an engine are the bits that do the pushing, like a cyclist's legs. Fine, but what pushes the pistons? The pictures on this page should give you a clue. The answer is the explosive power of FIRE. This is where a car stops being like the human body and starts getting a whole lot more interesting – and a whole lot more powerful. The chemical reactions that power your muscles are slow and gentle, but the chemical reactions that power a car are fast and violent. The fuel doesn't just burn: it **explodes**. Hundreds of times *every second*.

CRASH BANG WALLOP!

What a picture! The stupendous force of a massive petrol explosion sends two cars hurtling through the air like toys. Except this isn't actually possible. The explosion is completely fake – a stunt set up for a Hollywood movie. Cars can't explode like this: there just isn't enough oxygen in the fuel tank for the petrol to burn that quickly.

What actually *is* fire?
Fire is a high-speed chemical reaction happening right before your eyes. Oxygen from the air reacts with energy-rich molecules (like the molecules in petrol) to form new compounds that are given off as gases. The energy that was trapped in the fuel molecules escapes as heat and light, making the gases glow: a flame. The heat also makes the gases expand, and that can happen violently: an explosion. If you trap the exploding gas in a confined space, it creates a pushing force. And that's what pushes the pistons in an engine.

WARNING
EXPLOSIONS

Internal combustion

Every second about **300** tiny explosions happen in the engine, each one burning up just a *thousandth of a teaspoon* of petrol. These micro-doses of petrol are squirted into the cylinders as a spray and set alight by carefully timed electric sparks. The explosions happen right inside the engine's cylinders, on top of the pistons, and the **BLAST FORCE** pushes the pistons down. The crankshaft then swings round and pushes the pistons back up for the next stage in the cycle. Each piston makes 4 "strokes" (up or down movements) for every bang. The whole cycle for just one piston is shown below.

The pistons fit snugly into hollow cylinders in a large block of metal – the engine block. Fuel burns inside the cylinders (that's why it's called an *internal combustion engine*.)

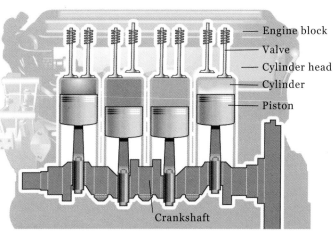

Engine block
Valve
Cylinder head
Cylinder
Piston
Crankshaft

The FOUR-STROKE CYCLE

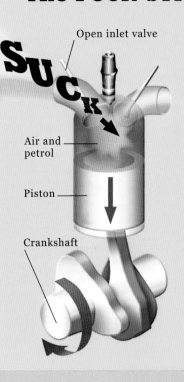

Open inlet valve
Air and petrol
Piston
Crankshaft

SUCK

SQUEEZE

Spark plug

BANG

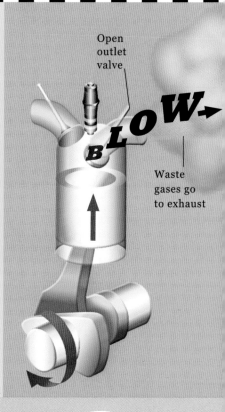

Open outlet valve

BLOW

Waste gases go to exhaust

Suck (down stroke): The piston moves down, sucking in air through the inlet valve. A tiny squirt of petrol is injected into the air.

Squeeze (up stroke): The inlet valve at the top closes, trapping everything inside. The piston moves up, squeezing the air and petrol tightly together.

Bang (down stroke): When the piston reaches the top, a carefully timed spark sets fire to the petrol. The petrol burns explosively, forcing the piston back down.

Blow (up stroke): Finally, the piston moves back up and pushes the burnt gases out of the outlet valve. These gases leave the car through the exhaust.

Revving it up

During one whole cycle of "suck, squeeze, bang, blow", the pistons move up and down twice, turning the crankshaft around twice as well. This all happens amazingly quickly. Next time you're in a car, look at the dashboard. Next to the speedometer is a smaller dial called the rev counter. It shows how fast the crankshaft is turning round, in revolutions per

RPM

minute (rpm). The numbers stand for thousands, so if the needle is on 5, the crankshaft is doing 5000 rpm, which works out as 83 revolutions per second! When the driver puts her or his foot down, the engine spins even faster and the needle climbs. If the engine goes too fast, the needle crosses the "redline". At these high revs, the engine generates such powerful forces that it can damage itself.

Pulling power

Cars are powered by the tiny explosions of petrol that happen deep inside the engine thousands of times a minute. The more petrol the engine can burn, and the quicker it can burn it, the faster the energy in petrol can be unleashed. The ***speed at which energy is unleashed*** is exactly what power is, and we measure it with a very old-fashioned unit: horsepower. If your car has a 135-horsepower engine, think of it as a cart being pulled by 135 invisible horses (but without all the mess that horses leave behind).

Average family car

A Scottish engineer and scientist called James Watt invented the term horsepower. Watt built steam engines and tried to sell them to people who were used to using horses, so he compared the power of his machines to the power of horses. But he bungled the calculations.

Now Watt have I done wrong???

The story goes that Watt based his sums on ponies, which could haul 220 lb of coal 100 feet up a mineshaft in 1 minute (22,000 pound feet per minute). Then he simply guessed – wrongly – that horses are 50% more powerful, giving us the figure of 33,000 pound-feet per minute for 1 horsepower. In reality, horses can't pull much more coal than ponies, so a real horse only has 0.7 horsepower. Fortunately scientists now use a better unit for power: the watt. No prizes for guessing who that's named after.

James Watt (1736-1819)

You can measure the horsepower of anything that uses energy, from a lightbulb to a space shuttle. There are actually at least five different definitions of horsepower, all confusingly different. Unsurprisingly, car manufacturers like to choose the one that makes their cars sound best, which of course leads to lots of arguing. Most scientists now prefer to measure power in Watts, which causes fewer disagreements.

Horsepower:	0.13	0.25	0.7	2

Watts:	100	200	520	1500

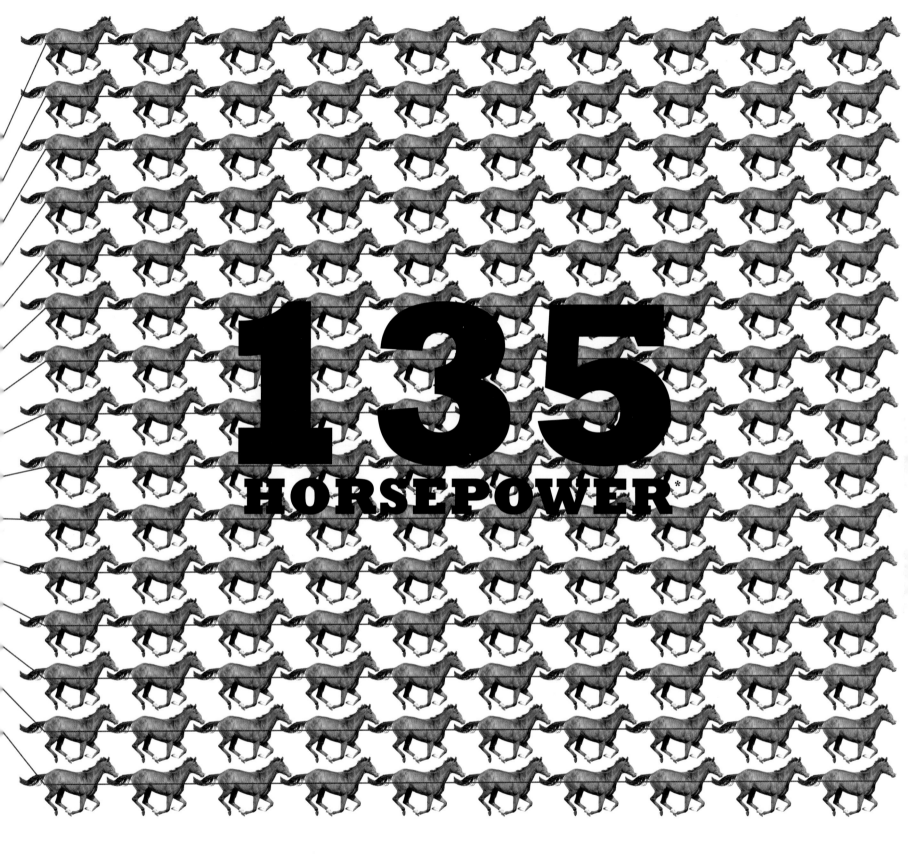

135
HORSEPOWER*

* Or 150 horsepower if you supercharge it.

4	60	135	900	27,000	15,000,000
3000	45,000	100,000	670,000	20 million	lots

SUPERPOWER

Option 1: Make the engine BIG

The bigger the engine, the more fuel it can swallow. The world's biggest truck is the Liebherr T282. It's the size of a small house and its engine is as big as a car. A typical car might take in 1.5 litres of air and petrol with each cycle, but the engine in this monster takes in 78 litres. Which makes it pretty powerful. And it needs to be: its job is to haul vast heaps of mining rubble, and it weighs over 500 tonnes fully laden.

Big engines can generate enormous pulling power for hauling loads, but there's a catch: they **weigh a lot**, which means they **slow the vehicle down**. The Liebherr has a top speed of only 40 mph (64 km/h) and a 0 to 60 time of never.

LIEBHERR

For sale
£2 million

LIEBHERR
MINING POWER

Top speed: 40 mph (64 km/h)

0–60 mph (0–97 km/h): never

Miles per gallon: 0.3

Empty vehicle weight: 201 tonnes

Power: 3500 horsepower

Power is all about burning fuel quickly, and you can make an engine do that in different ways. One way is to make the engine huge, so it can gulp in more fuel with each turn of the crankshaft. Another way is to make it spin faster. These two routes to superpower are used in very different kinds of vehicles.

Option 2: Make the engine *fast*

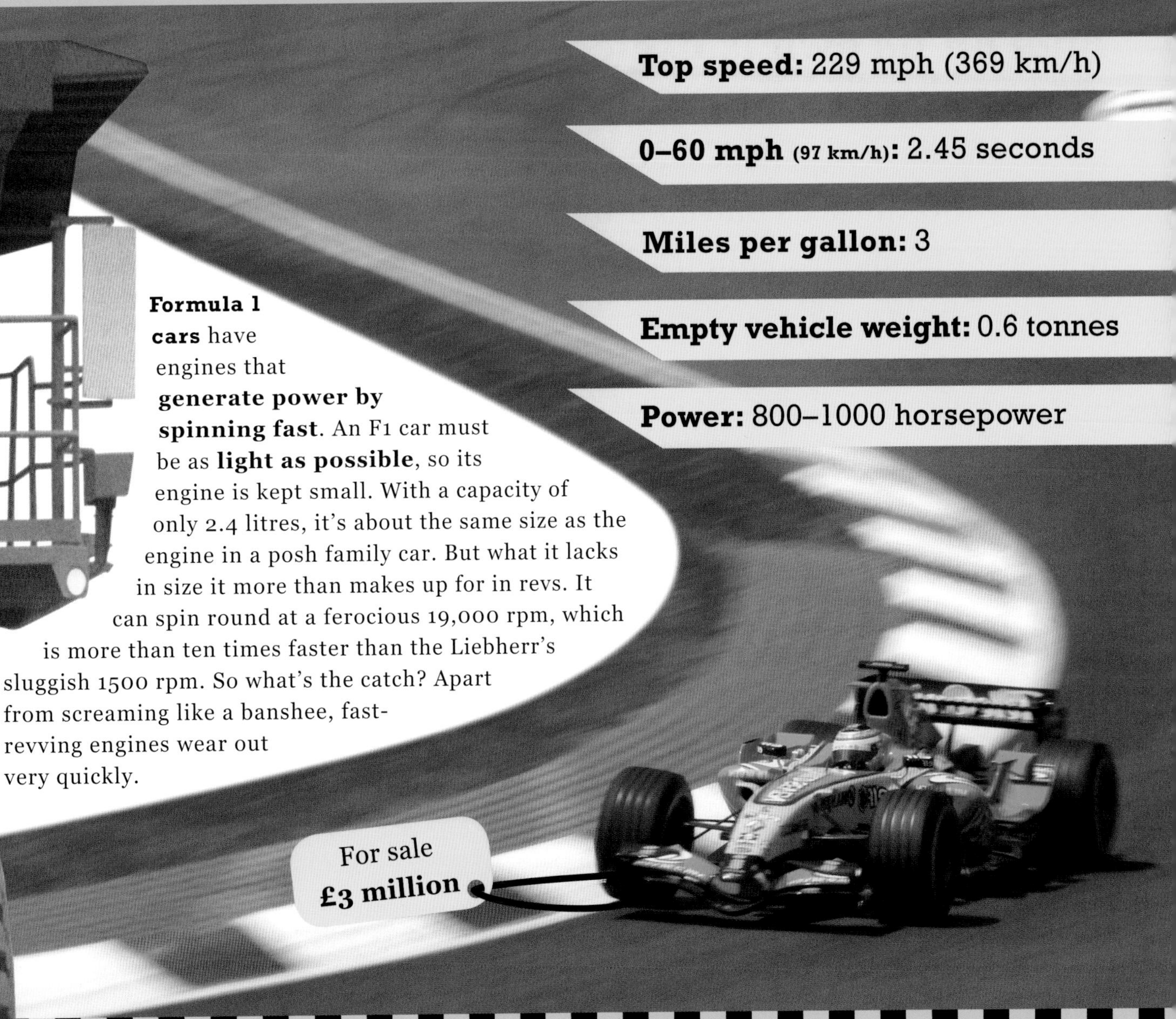

Top speed: 229 mph (369 km/h)

0–60 mph (97 km/h)**:** 2.45 seconds

Miles per gallon: 3

Empty vehicle weight: 0.6 tonnes

Power: 800–1000 horsepower

Formula 1 cars have engines that **generate power by spinning fast**. An F1 car must be as **light as possible**, so its engine is kept small. With a capacity of only 2.4 litres, it's about the same size as the engine in a posh family car. But what it lacks in size it more than makes up for in revs. It can spin round at a ferocious 19,000 rpm, which is more than ten times faster than the Liebherr's sluggish 1500 rpm. So what's the catch? Apart from screaming like a banshee, fast-revving engines wear out very quickly.

For sale
£3 million

Can you talk the torque?

Engineers compare the brute strength of different engines by measuring a mysterious thing called torque. It sounds complicated but it's actually very simple: torque is just a twisting force. When you use a spanner to loosen a bolt, the spanner generates a torque on the bolt. The longer the spanner, the greater the torque. The pistons in a car generate torque on the crankshaft in the same way. As with the spanner, the bigger the pistons and the cranks, the greater the torque. The massive pistons in the dumper truck engine produce a stupendous amount of torque, which gives the truck enormous pulling power even when the engine is only ticking over. The Formula 1 car is the opposite. Its lightweight engine has small pistons that produce little torque – barely more than a good road car. So to unleash the engine's full power, the driver has to rev it up to the max. The two routes to power can be summed up in a neat equation:

power = torque x revs

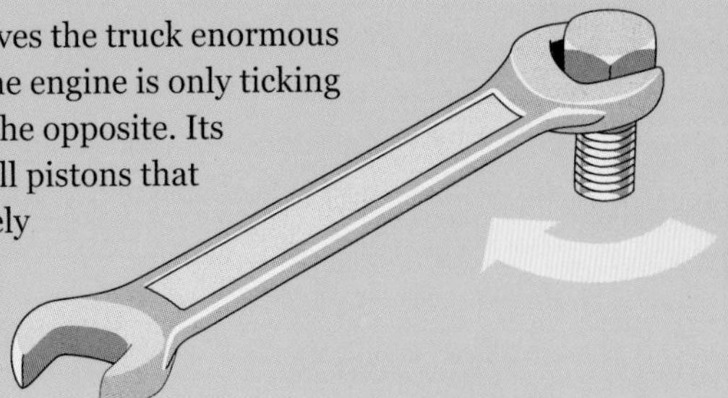

21

Step on the gas (or air)

Fuel on its own is useless – it won't burn and release energy unless you add the same magic ingredient that keeps you going: **OXYGEN.** And to get all the oxygen it needs, an engine must gulp in a truly vast quantity of air: about 9000 times as much air by volume as petrol. Your lungs breathe in about 6 litres of fresh air a minute, but a powerful car needs thousands of times as much.

25 litres of air per minute

75 litres of air per minute

3000 litres of air per minute

Citroen C3

The accelerator pedal in a car is really an "air pedal". It works by opening a valve called the throttle, which lets more air into the engine, which also indirectly increases how much fuel enters the engine. With more fuel and air entering the engine, the explosions in the cyclinders become more forceful and the pistons are pushed harder, making the engine spin faster. The revs increase, and so the wheels spin faster too, making the car accelerate.

Power boosters

The reason big engines are more powerful than small engines is because they can hold more air. But you can also cram more air molecules into the cylinders by squeezing the air in more tightly. This is what superchargers and turbos do. These devices are basically air compressors that push more air into the cylinders, which in turn causes more fuel to be drawn in too. The result is more powerful explosions – and therefore a whole lot more torque to play with.

18,000 litres
of air
per minute

12,000 litres
of air
per minute

Bugatti Veyron

Formula 1 car

Superchargers
These are also called "blowers". Unlike a turbo, a supercharger is driven by a belt connected to the crankshaft. As the car speeds up, the supercharger makes a high-pitched whine that gets louder and louder – which is all part of the fun.

Turbochargers
Turbochargers are driven by hot air rushing out of the car's exhaust. Some types of turbo kick in suddenly as you rev up the engine, causing a sudden rush of speed and adrenaline.

Nitrous oxide
Nitrous oxide is a gas that breaks down inside the engine, boosting the amount of oxygen within the cylinders and making the combustion more powerful. It's often used in drag racing, but some people fit nitrous kits on ordinary road cars to boost horsepower.

Piston power

As we've seen, the pistons in an engine do the same job as your legs when you're riding a bike. But you only have two legs. Imagine how much more powerful your bike would be if you had four or eight legs instead (though saying that, you'd need a pretty weird bike). Well cars can have as many pistons as they like, within reason. And the number and the shape in which they're arranged both have a big influence on the power and personality of the car.

This is tricky with 11 legs!

Single

Engines with a single cylinder don't have enough power for cars, but they're fine for lawnmowers and mopeds. Because there are no other pistons to smooth out the bangs, they produce a lot of vibration.

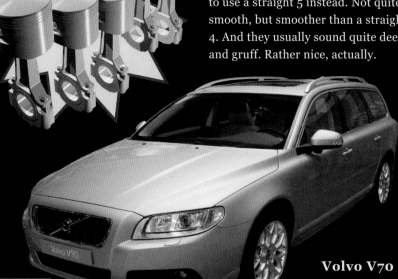

Lawnmower

V twin

Motorbikes tend to have 1-4 cylinders, but the Harley-Davidson has two arranged in a V. The pistons are large and don't move up and down very quickly. As a result, the Harley engine makes a distinctive *thump thump* noise that gives the bike loads of character. The engine shakes a lot, but that's part of the character too.

Harley-Davidson Shovelhead

Straight 5

Straight 6 engines are very well balanced, but they're long and difficult to fit under the bonnet. The answer is to use a straight 5 instead. Not quite as smooth, but smoother than a straight 4. And they usually sound quite deep and gruff. Rather nice, actually.

Volvo V70

V6

Instead of arranging six cylinders in a line you can put three each side of a V. This makes a nice compact engine. A V6 is not quite as smooth as a straight 6 but has bags of character and sounds very nice.

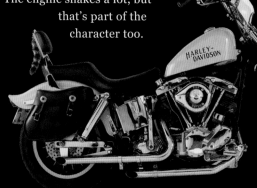

Audi TT V6 Quattro

Capacity

The amount of air an engine can fit into all its cylinders in one go is called **engine capacity**, and it's a good clue to the engine's power. It's measured in litres, so when someone says their car is a "two litre whatever" or a "something one-point-eight", they're telling you how much air their car's engine can hold.

Shape

The **cylinders** in an engine are arranged to fire in pairs or one after the other, which helps the engine run more smoothly. The shape of their arrangement also matters. In simple engines the cylinders are lined up, but this can magnify vibrations. Better to arrange them in opposite pairs, so they cancel each other out, or in a **V-shape**.

Straight 4

Most small family cars have straight (in-line) four-cylinder engines, usually up to about 2.0 litres in size. They're quite smooth, compact and do a very good job. They do sound a bit boring though.

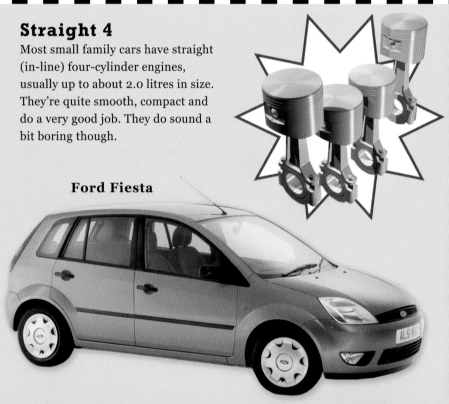

Ford Fiesta

Flat 4

The famous Beetle used a flat 4 engine. These are often called boxer engines because the pistons move like boxers' fists. One of the advantages of a flat 4 is that they can be mounted low in the car, which keeps the weight low down – good for handling. Flat engines make a very distinctive noise, especially when they're made with even more cylinders. Porsche's 911 has a flat 6, and Ferrari even made a flat 12.

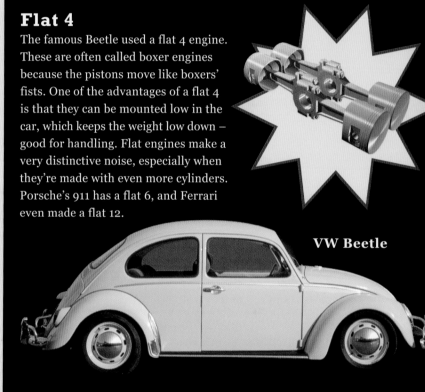

VW Beetle

V8

Car enthusiasts love V8s. They're big – usually over 3.5 litres – and powerful. But it's the noise that gets everybody excited, especially if the car's silencers aren't very effective. A big V8 is almost like a living thing: it shakes and growls, and when you rev it the hairs on the back of your neck stand up.

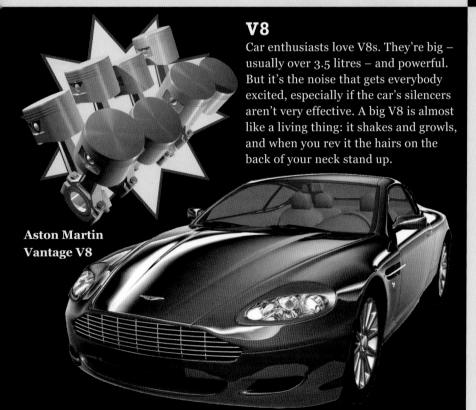

Aston Martin Vantage V8

Wankel Rotary

The rotary engine is very interesting. The pistons are triangular and move around inside an odd-shaped cylinder. Only Mazda uses these engines. They're very smooth, compact, and produce a lot of power. Without silencing they're incredibly loud, with a unique sound like carpet being torn. They also tend to be a bit thirsty for fuel.

Mazda RX8

Bugatti Veyron

£850,000 o.n.o.

Top speed:
253 mph (407 km/h)

0–60 mph: 2.46 sec
(0–97 km/h)

Engine: 8-litre W16 with
4 turbochargers

Power:
1001 brake horsepower

Miles per gallon: 12
(normal) 2.5 mpg at full throttle

MONSTER ENGINE

Everything about the Bugatti Veyron is mind-boggling, including its price. Let's start with the engine: a 1001-brake-horsepower monster that takes up a massive space in the centre of the car. We've already seen how the pistons and crankshaft are laid out in an engine, and how some engines have only one piston and some have as many as eight. Well, the Veyron has 16 pistons and two crankshafts, with the pistons arranged in a W shape. Volkswagen (which owns Bugatti) built the engine by using parts from two of its 4.0-litre V8 engines, which is why the Veyron has a monster 8.0 litre capacity.

The Veyron's huge engine is connected to all four wheels (four-wheel drive), allowing the car to put all its power down without spinning them.

The 16 cylinders pump up and down in a coordinated cycle that makes the engine luxuriously smooth.

The MONSTER ENGINE with a beast of a price tag

We've seen how a turbocharger is used to cram more air (and hence more fuel) into an engine to increase the power – well, the Veyron has four of them. In fact, the Veyron has more of everything, including gears, of which it has seven. The gearbox is semi-automatic: it's like a conventional manual gearbox except that the clutches (yes, it has two) are operated automatically and the gears are engaged by flicking paddles on the steering wheel, like those on a Formula 1 car. When driving at 250 mph (402 km/h) it's quite a good idea to have good brakes. The Veyron has. The brake discs are made of carbon fibre and the front ones are squeezed by pads operated by eight pistons (most cars have only four). Bugatti says that the Veyron will come to a stop from **249 mph** (401 km/h) in under **10 seconds**. Hold on to your hat!

When its speed hits 137 mph (220 km/h), the Veyron's body lowers automatically to reduce air pressure under the car.

The streamlined shape allows air to flow smoothly over the surface.

Aerodynamics

Most vehicles that go faster than 250 mph (402 km/h) are called aeroplanes. As you can see, the Veyron is clearly a car. To stop the car taking off at top speed like a plane, the Veyron's designers had to get the car's shape exactly right so that the wind pushes it down onto the road, creating "downforce". You can find out more about downforce on page 50.

The rear spoiler creates up to 0.4 tonnes of downforce to press the car onto the road.

Black gold

Petrol and diesel come from *petroleum* – a slimy black substance found deep underground. So where does petroleum come from?

Recipe for crude oil

Let's suppose you're going to make your own supply of petroleum. It's not especially difficult, it's just a little time-consuming. Well, *very* time-consuming actually. Here's a step-by-step guide on how to do it.

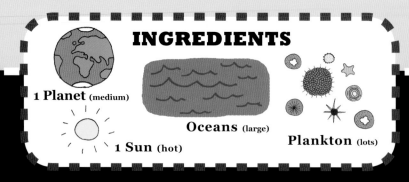

INGREDIENTS

1 Planet (medium)   Oceans (large)   1 Sun (hot)   Plankton (lots)

IN THE BEGINNING...

1 Take one medium planet. Add water to create oceans. Place under a hot Sun.

Plankton

Yum! Plankton!

2 Add a generous sprinkling of plankton to the water. Leave them to multiply in the sunlight for many millions of years.

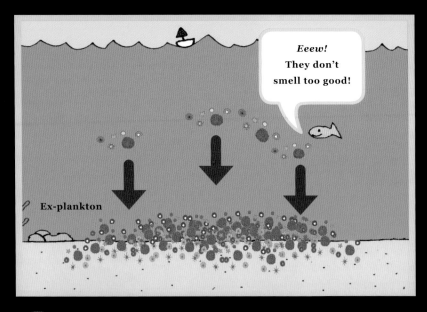

Eeew! They don't smell too good!

Ex-plankton

3 When plankton die, let them sink onto the sandy sea floor and turn into a layer of disgusting slime.

RIP

4 Now bury the plankton under a layer of sand. Do this slowly over millions of years.

The petrol and diesel we put in cars are called **_fossil fuels_** because they really are made from fossils. When your mum or dad fills up the tank, they're pouring in the ancient, rotten remains of billions of dead sea organisms. The remains were once plankton – invisibly tiny plants that floated near the sea surface, minding their own business and soaking up the energy from sunlight – just so you could use that energy millions of years in the future for a drive.

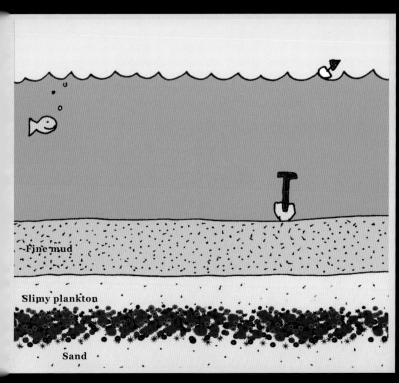

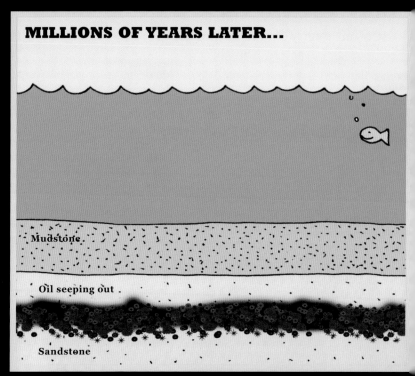

5 Add a layer of very fine mud on top of the sand. Take a break and come back in 100 million years or so.

6 The sand has turned into rock (sandstone) and so has the mud (mudstone). Oil from the plankton is seeping up into the sandstone but the mudstone traps it. Take another long break.

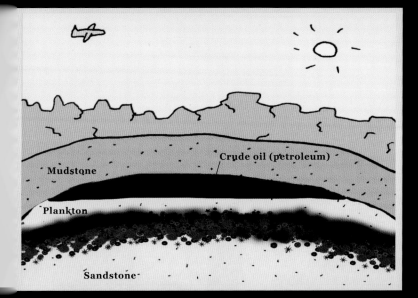

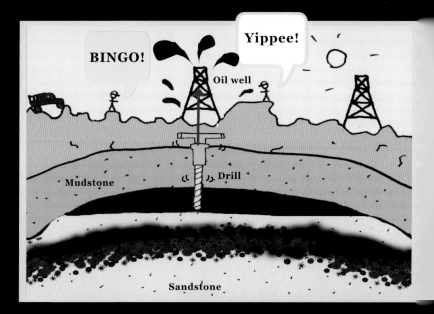

7 The ocean has gone and the sea floor is now land. Oil from the plankton has formed an upside-down "pool" in the sandstone, trapped by the mudstone – an oil reservoir.

8 Buy a very big drill and make a hole down to the sandstone. Bingo – you've struck oil! You're rich. Buy yourself a Bugatti Veyron.

Making petrol

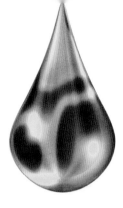

The **crude oil** that comes out of the ground is slippery and black. It has to be separated into its different parts, called "**fractions**", to give us petrol and diesel.

From this... ... **to this!**

crude oil

petrol

Crude oil is actually a mixture of hundreds of different chemicals, but all of these chemicals have something important in common – they're all made of chains of **carbon atoms** with **hydrogen atoms** stuck on the side. We call them *hydrocarbons.*

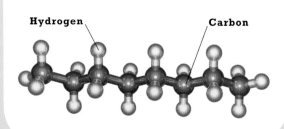

Hydrogen   Carbon

Chain reactions

To make petrol, the mixture has to be sorted out into chains of similar lengths. It's fairly easy to do this – you just boil the crude oil and pass the vapours through a tower fitted with trays at different heights. As they hit the trays, the vapours condense back into liquids, and are drained off. The longest carbon chains come off at the bottom, forming a thick, treacly liquid used for tarmac. The shortest chains are gases and rise to the top. Nearly every fraction is useful.

Crude Oil

HEAT boils the oil

Petrol is packed with energy. Pound for pound, it contains about three times as much energy as sugar, five times as much as wood, and nearly 200 times as much energy as the same weight of batteries.

Length of carbon chain

FRACTIONING TOWER

1-4

carbon atoms

5-12

12-15

12-20

20-50

20-70

70+

ARE WE GOING TO RUN OUT?

The world currently uses about 87 million barrels of crude oil a day. Demand is rising as developing nations industrialize and need fuel for cars and power stations. Estimates put known reserves at 1,200 billion barrels, with perhaps as much again still to be discovered. This could provide us with oil until 2100, but we may have to make oil from other types of hydrocarbon deposits – tar sands, oil shales, or even coal if supplies get really low.

What it makes

Petroleum gas

World production: 590 million tonnes per year.

Short-chain gases are used by the chemical industry to make plastics, or liquefied and kept under pressure in canisters as fuel.

Petrol

World production: 900 million tonnes per year.

Petrol is a blend of short-chain liquid hydrocarbons that all have a lower boiling point than water. If you spill petrol it evaporates very quickly.

Jet fuel

World production: 235 million tonnes per year.

Kerosene, or paraffin, is a thin, clear liquid used in jet engines. Also used for portable stoves and heaters.

Diesel

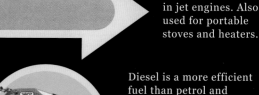

World production: 1,200 million tonnes per year.

Diesel is a more efficient fuel than petrol and produces more energy when it is burned. It also produces less carbon dioxide, but contains higher levels of other pollutants, such as sulphur and nitrogen oxides.

Lubricating oil

World production: 40 million tonnes per year.

Lubricating oils are used to reduce friction and wear between moving surfaces. Motor oil is used to protect engine parts.

Fuel oil

World production: 610 million tonnes per year.

Fuel oils have a wide range of uses. Lighter oils contain more diesel and are used in ships and tractors, or as heating oil. Heavy oils are burned in power station furnaces and industrial boilers.

Bitumen

World production: 105 million tonnes per year.

Bitumen, or asphalt, is a sticky, black semi-solid that is mixed with small stones and used for road surfaces.

LAWS OF *motion*

MAGNETISM

All the power in the world won't budge a car unless that car can use its power to generate *FORCES*. The idea of forces may sound a little complicated, but nothing could actually be simpler. A force is just a **push** or a **pull**. Wherever there's action and movement, forces are sure to be involved.

Whether you're riding a bike, kicking a ball, or turning a page of this book, you're using forces to make things move. Usually you have to touch something to apply a force to it, but there are some forces that work from a distance, such as gravity and magnetism. Planet Earth uses the invisible force of gravity to pull everything towards it (though nobody has the faintest idea how or why). Try letting go of this book: Earth will pull it off you immediately without even touching it. And without even asking.

GRAVITY

PUSHING

PULLING

NEWTON'S LAWS

The first person to really figure out forces was the English scientist Sir Isaac Newton (1642–1727). Newton was a foul-tempered oddball who hated people and spent an awful lot of time alone, carrying out weird experiments and thinking endlessly about things like gravity. Peculiar though he undoubtedly was, he was also brilliant, and he figured out how gravity controls the movement of the planets. His theory hinged on three simple laws that explain how forces make *everything* move.

Newton's laws

1
"An object that isn't being **pushed** or **pulled** by a force either stays still or keeps moving in a straight line at a constant speed."

2
"Forces make things **accelerate**. The bigger the force, and the lighter the object, the greater the acceleration."

3
"Every **action** has an equal and opposite **reaction**."

Newton's first law says that a moving object will carry on moving forever, in a straight line at a constant speed, unless some kind of force stops it. It took the genius of Newton to discover this law because it's usually not obvious that it's happening: moving objects are nearly always being tugged by forces like friction and gravity, which get in the way. But when a car loses grip on a wet road, friction is much weaker and the car glides along in a straight line, showing Newton's law at work.

Newton's second law means that forces make things move or change the way they're moving. In everyday language "acceleration" means going faster, but to a scientist it can mean three things: speeding up, slowing down (negative acceleration), or changing direction. The second bit of the law simply means that lightweight things need less force to move than heavy things. And that's why small sports cars have better acceleration than big lorries.

"Coming first is a doddle when you get to write the rules!"

Newton's third law means that forces (Newton called them "actions") always come in opposite pairs. Think what happens when you kick a football: your foot applies a force to the ball and makes it move; but the ball also pushes back on your foot, applying a force that you feel pressing against your shoe and skin. The third law explains how rocket engines work: these engines push burning gases out backwards with a powerful force. As a result, an equal and opposite force pushes the rocket-car forwards.

MAGNIFYING FORCES

Cars use the energy released by fuel to generate powerful **FORCES**. The twisting force, or *torque*, that turns the crankshaft (and the wheels) is the most obvious force at work in a car, but there are loads of others. Some of the most important ones come from the driver, whose body generates the forces that steer and brake the car. Puny though the driver may be, the forces he or she produces are still handy because you can **magnify** them. Scientists call anything that magnifies a force a "machine". Think of the jack your dad uses to lift his car. He probably can't lift a car on his own, but the jack makes it easy because it magnifies the force of his arms.

the INCLINED PLANE

It takes a huge force just to lift a car off the ground, so how on Earth can you lift it to the top of a mountain? Easy: find a gently sloping road and drive up. The road turns the mountain into a ramp (an inclined plane). The engine can push you from the bottom to the top more easily because you're driving up an angle. The gentler the incline, the easier it is.

the LEVER

Some of the simplest machines are based on LEVERS. A lever is a stiff bar with a fixed point called a pivot – like a seesaw. When you push one end, it rotates around the pivot. Here's the clever bit: one end of a lever is longer than the other. If you push the long end, the short end magnifies the force (but moves a shorter distance). The pedals in a car use double levers that magnify the force from the driver's feet.

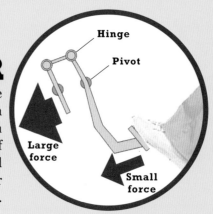

Hinge

Pivot

Large force

Small force

Machines that magnify forces might appear to give you something for nothing, but there's a catch: the magnified force moves a much shorter distance than the input force. Think of your dad's jack again: he pumps the handle over and over again, but the car only moves up a tiny bit each time. What you gain in force, you pay in distance.

Gears

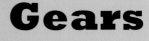

What do you do if your car's engine doesn't produce much torque, but you need lots of torque at the wheels to pull a heavy load or climb a hill? Easy: magnify the torque by changing gear. Gears are just cogs. Join a small one to a big one and you multiply the turning force (torque). You can find out more about gears on the next page.

In cars with rack-and-pinion steering, a pair of cunning gears at the end of the steering column turn rotation into straight-line motion to move the wheels.

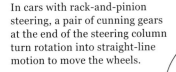

Pinion

Rack

Weak force from arms

Magnified force around axle

the WHEEL

If you hold the outside of a wheel and turn it, the wheel's axle will turn with a powerful torque, magnifying the force of your arms. This is exactly what steering wheels do. They magnify the force from the driver's puny arms to produce enough force to turn the wheels. These days most cars make the job even easier by boosting the steering force with a bit of power from the engine (power steering).

Hydraulics

Pivot **Cylinder**

Brake pedal

Brake fluid

Brake disc

Brake pad

When you stamp on the brakes, you need force from your leg to be carried rapidly to all four wheels at the same time. You also need the force boosting greatly to give you instant stopping power. Imagine all the complex levers you'd need to carry force from the brake pedal to the back wheels. A better solution in this case is to use hydraulics – a way of carrying forces through fluid-filled pipes. Step on the brakes and you pump fluid through a cylinder, down a narrow pipe, to the brakes. The fluid pushes the brake pads hard against the brake disc, which stops the wheel with friction. The piston at the brake disc is much wider than the one at the brake pedal, so it hugely magnifies your pushing force, as in the example below.

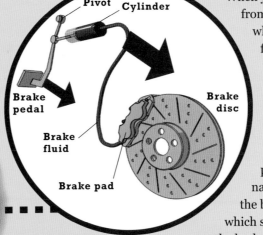

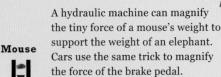

A hydraulic machine can magnify the tiny force of a mouse's weight to support the weight of an elephant. Cars use the same trick to magnify the force of the brake pedal.

Mouse

Getting in GEAR

Why do you need gears?

The gears on a bike allow your legs to pump up and down at a comfortable speed all the time, even though the speed of the wheels changes enormously. A car's gears do exactly the same job (think of the pistons as legs). And just like a bike's gears, a car's gears can magnify torque – giving the wheels the powerful force they need to climb hills or get you going in the first place.

What are gears?

Gears are simply cogs – wheels with teeth. If you connect a small gear to a big gear with ten times as many teeth, the small gear will make ten turns for every one turn of the big gear. Now connect the small gear to the car's engine and the big gear to the wheels. Bingo! You've solved the problem of getting a fast-revving engine to turn the wheels slowly.

One engine, many cars

Using gears is like having many cars in one. You change gear to help your engine match the driving conditions, using your engine's power to create either lots of torque (to start moving or climb hills) or lots of speed (for motorway cruising).

20%

1st gear

It takes huge force to get a car moving. In 1st gear, the wheels turn slowly but with masses of torque – ideal to get the car moving.

From engine — *wheels*

2nd gear

Once you're moving, you need a bit more speed and a bit less torque. Choose 2nd gear: the wheels can now spin faster. But they still have plenty of torque – handy if you need a burst of acceleration.

From engine — *To wheels*

1st gear

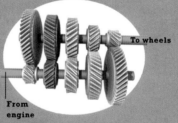

Oh dear – you've come to a steep hill and slowed right down. You now need a lot more torque at the wheels again for the car to pull itself uphill. Back down to first gear please.

From engine — *wheels*

Differential gears

Inner wheel goes shorter distance and slower

Differential

Outer wheel goes further and faster

There's a second, mini-gearbox tucked between the wheels. Shaped like a pumpkin, it's called a differential, and its main job is to help you go round corners. When a car rounds a bend, the outer wheels have to travel further than the inner ones, so they have to turn faster. The cogs in the differential let a car's inner and outer wheels turn at different speeds. This is great for normal driving but there's a snag. If one wheel loses grip by riding into slippery mud or getting stuck in the air, the differential will let it spin like crazy and waste all the power. Off-roaders get round this problem by using cleverer differentials that direct power to whichever wheel has got the best grip.

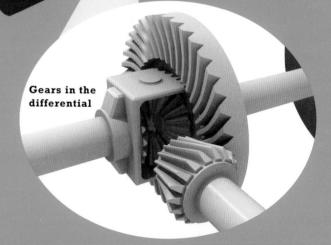

Axles turn wheels

Driveshaft carries power from engine

Gears in the differential

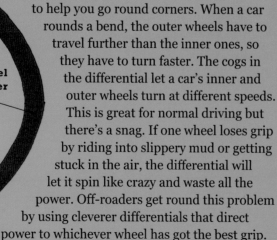

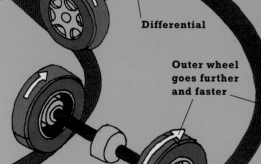

Inside the gearbox

A car's gearbox contains pairs of cogs of varying sizes. One row sits on a shaft driven by the engine, and the others sit on a shaft that drives the wheels. At any moment, only one pair is clamped firmly to the rotating shafts and therefore carrying the engine's power. By using the gearstick, you can choose which pair does the job: a big cog connected to a little cog, a little cog connected to a big cog, or something in between.

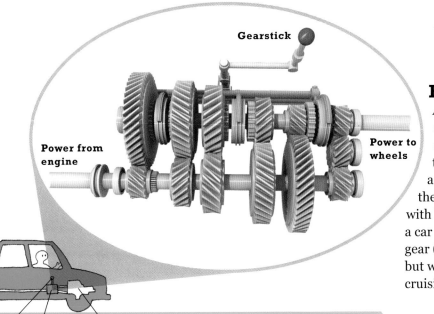

Gearstick

Power from engine

Power to wheels

Gearstick   Gearbox   Engine

Feel the force

As well as changing the speed at which a car's spinning parts are spinning, gears change the turning force – the torque. When a car is in a low gear (1st or 2nd), the wheels turn round slowly but with lots of torque – ideal for pulling a car uphill. When the car is in a high gear (3rd or 4th), the wheels spin fast but with little torque, which is fine for cruising at speed along motorways.

40

60

2nd gear

Heading downhill, you don't really need any torque because gravity is doing all the work. But stay in a low gear anyway because it's safer – it will stop the wheels spinning too quickly.

To wheels

From engine

3rd gear

Back on the straight, you can accelerate. Switch to 3rd, which allows your wheels to spin a lot faster.

To wheels

From engine

4th gear

You hit the motorway. Now you want the wheels to spin fast rather than with lots of torque so choose 4th or higher.

To wheels

From engine

MAKE A SPUD GEARBOX

You will need:
- A thick piece of cardboard (an old packing carton is perfect)
- Cocktail sticks or sharp pencils
- Pastry cutters of various sizes (but with roughly the same sized teeth) or a table knife
- A few potatoes of different sizes (as round as possible)

1. Cut slices about 0.5 cm (0.2 in) thick from the middle of each potato. You want your slices to be as round as possible. Use a small jar lid as a guide to help you trim them to a more circular shape.

2. Press out some "gears" of different sizes using the pastry cutters, or cut

equal-sized notches around the edges of the potato circles.

3. Mount your gears onto the cardboard by pushing the cocktail sticks or pencils through the potato slices. Arrange the gears so their teeth mesh together. If you turn one wheel, you should find the others turn too. If you make your gears the same size, they should all turn at the same speed.

4. Experiment with gears of different sizes. Try to turn a small gear with a big one – the smaller one should turn faster because it has fewer teeth. If you turn a large gear with a smaller one, the larger wheel should turn more slowly.

5. Don't worry if your gearbox doesn't work. You can always fry it to make chips and eat it for dinner!

Fantastic. We've dug a hole in the ground, found some oil, and we've turned it into petrol. We've also designed a really amazing engine that's got more horsepower than the Grand National horse race. Let's go fast.

But hold on, because there's more to going fast than just power. For starters there's this thing called drag – the force of the air holding you back – and it's not good news for speed. Then there's weight: too much of it will slow you down even more, as you'd find out if you tried running with a dining table strapped to your back.

Loads of different forces are involved in the science of speed, and to break records we need to understand them. Racing drivers, who go fast for a living, really need to understand the science of speed because otherwise they'll be slow. And then they're called losers.

Speed

The need for

What is it about speed that human beings (and apparently dogs) seem to love so much? Every time people have invented a new way of getting around – whether it's driving, cycling, water-skiing, or standing in a sack and hopping – they've turned it into a race to see who can go fastest. Maybe it's just the buzz of winning, or the thrill of the wind in your face. Or maybe it's just that, without any help, human beings are actually *incredibly slow*. Put us in a race with almost any other animal (snails and tortoises excepted), and we'd lose.

Top speeds:

Thrust SSC land-speed record

Bugatti Veyron

Ford Focus

Cheetah — 62 mph (100km/h)

Model-T Ford — 45 mph (72 km/h)

Racehorse — 43 mph (69 km/h)

Hare — 40 mph (64 km/h)

Crow — 30 mph (48 km/h)

Person walking — 4 mph (6.5 km/h)

Tortoise — 0.2 mph (0.3 km/h)

Snail — 0.03 mph (0.05 km/h)

Why are we so slow?

When apes gave up being apes and climbed out of trees to become us, they opted for a clunky two-legged style of walking instead of the normal mammalian four-legged style. Bad choice (well, bad for speed). The average human now can't run much faster than 10 mph (16 km/h), which – compared to horses, dogs, hares, lions, bears, bison, buffaloes, and pretty much everything – is frankly embarrassing. Solution: invent cars.

SPEED

SPEED = DISTANCE ÷ TIME

The speed something has is the distance it travels in a certain amount of time. You can work out a car's average speed by dividing the total distance it travels by the total time it takes. But how do you work out a car's speed at one particular moment in time? The answer is in the box.

763 mph (1228 km/h)

253 mph (407 km/h)

125 mph (225 km/h)

ANSWERS
Speed question: Look at the speedometer, of course!
Velocity question: Zero. Think about it.
Kinetic energy question: You have four times as much energy. Because of the little "squared" symbol in that equation, the amount of kinetic energy in a moving car increases enormously even when speed only rises a little. And it's the amount of kinetic energy a moving car has that determines how severe a crash will be. This is why crashing at high speeds is such a very bad idea.

VELOCITY

Scientists sometimes use the word velocity instead of speed. But it isn't quite the same: velocity is your speed *in a particular direction*. So if you drive north at 50 mph (80 km/h) for an hour, then drive back south at the same speed for an hour, your average speed is 50, but what's your average velocity? The answer is in the box.

Time machines

100 years

260 days

8 and bit days

35 hours

A car is a time machine. You can use its *speed* to get somewhere more quickly than it would otherwise take, saving you time. Imagine you could walk all the way round Earth in a straight line without resting. It would take you 260 days at walking speed, but a car would cut that to 8 days, saving you 252 days for lounging by the pool when you reach your destination. In theory, the Thrust SSC jet car could make the trip in 35 hours. But it would need rather a lot of fuel: half a million gallons, which is 50 tankers-full.

Ford Focus

Thrust SSC jet car

KINETIC ENERGY

Moving objects have what we call *kinetic energy*. And as you'll probably guess, the faster you're going, the more kinetic energy you have. But if you double your speed, you don't simply double your energy, because this is how the equation works:

$$\text{kinetic energy} = \tfrac{1}{2} mv^2,$$

(m is mass, v is velocity). So if you double your speed, can you guess how much your kinetic energy increases? Answer in box.

Acceleration

You might think that speed is the ultimate thrill, but a high top speed is not actually what makes a car exciting to drive. A better measure of thrill-value is how quickly a car can get up to speed. In other words, it's not how fast you go that counts, *it's how fast your fastness changes*. And that's what acceleration is all about.

Measuring acceleration

Scientists measure acceleration with a very confusing unit: "metres per second per second". In the world of cars, we use a much simpler yardstick: the time a car takes to sprint from 0 to 60 mph (97 km/h). Only top supercars can do this in less than 4 seconds, and the current record-holder among road cars is the Bugatti Veyron, with an astonishing 0 to 60 time of 2.46 seconds. But any car with a 0 to 60 time of 6 seconds or less will give you a shot of adrenaline when you put your foot down. An average family car gets to 60 in about 10 seconds.

Honda Civic

0-60 in 10 seconds

Drag racing

Dragsters are the fastest accelerating vehicles on Earth, capable of screaming from 0 to 330 mph (530 km/h) in 4.45 seconds. Not even the space shuttle accelerates that fast. Their enormous engines generate up to 6700 horsepower (as much power as 30 Porsche Boxsters) and produce deafening vibrations that register up to 3.9 on the Richter earthquake scale. All that power goes to the rear tyres, which are gigantic for maximum grip (otherwise the engine's power would simply make them spin). Needless to say, dragsters are pretty dangerous. And to drive one, you have to be quite mad and very brave.

0-330 mph in 4.45 seconds

MÄKELÄ
PATOHARJ

"It's the speed of the speed that you need to succeed!"

Feel the force

To understand why acceleration *feels* exciting, we have to go back to Newton's laws. Forgotten them already? Never mind, here's the first one again:

"An object that isn't being pushed or pulled by a force either stays still or keeps moving in a straight line at a steady speed."

This law tells us that sitting still and moving in a straight line at a constant speed are actually not that different. That's why you can play cards in a plane or a train without the cards flying away at hundreds of miles an hour. You just can't *feel* the speed. Now for the second law again:

"Forces make objects accelerate. The greater the force or the lighter the object, the greater the acceleration."

This law tells you that acceleration is always associated with forces. When a car accelerates like the clappers, you *feel* a powerful force pushing you back into the seat. The force goes right through your body and affects every internal organ. It squeezes your lungs around your heart, it pushes your stomach against your spine, and it even squashes your eyes a bit. And all of that makes you feel like you're *really* moving.

Terminal velocity

Skydivers leap out of planes but then wait a whole minute before opening their parachutes. With nothing to stop gravity tugging them to Earth, they accelerate like rocks. But after a few seconds, they hit a magical speed – around 125 mph (200 km/h) – where they stop accelerating. They've reached what scientists call terminal velocity. So why does this happen?

The answer is that gravity isn't the only force acting on them. As they speed up, they face an increasingly powerful force from the air rushing past: **drag**. The drag force eventually balances gravity, and so the skydiver stops accelerating (but they don't stop falling). The same thing happens with cars. At high speeds, the force of drag becomes as strong as the force of the engine, and a car cannot accelerate any further – it has reached its top speed.

"Only 330 miles an hour? What a drag."

Small **is good**

The more power a car has, the faster it can *ACCELERATE* – and the more thrilling the drive. But power isn't everything. What's just as important is **weight** (or to be a bit more precise, **mass**. Mass is how much "stuff" there is in something, and it only becomes weight when gravity pulls on it.)

⮕ BIG vs small – on your marks!

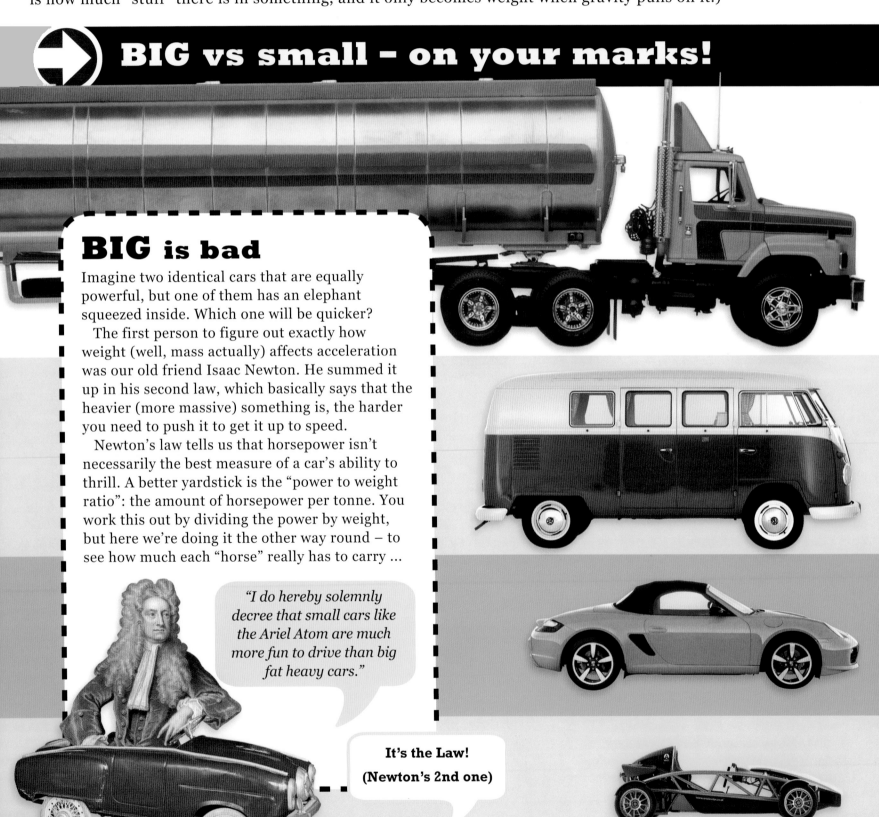

BIG is bad

Imagine two identical cars that are equally powerful, but one of them has an elephant squeezed inside. Which one will be quicker?

The first person to figure out exactly how weight (well, mass actually) affects acceleration was our old friend Isaac Newton. He summed it up in his second law, which basically says that the heavier (more massive) something is, the harder you need to push it to get it up to speed.

Newton's law tells us that horsepower isn't necessarily the best measure of a car's ability to thrill. A better yardstick is the "power to weight ratio": the amount of horsepower per tonne. You work this out by dividing the power by weight, but here we're doing it the other way round – to see how much each "horse" really has to carry ...

"I do hereby solemnly decree that small cars like the Ariel Atom are much more fun to drive than big fat heavy cars."

It's the Law!
(Newton's 2nd one)

Being quick off the mark isn't the only advantage to being small...

- As well as accelerating like the clappers, small cars decelerate and **stop quickly** in emergencies.
- Small cars **corner more easily**, sharply, and safely, making them more exciting to drive.
- They use **less fuel** than heavy cars, which makes them cheaper to run and less polluting.
- And when they break down, they're a whole lot easier to push!

Acceleration

0–60 mph (97 km/h) in ...

MILK TANKER

A lorry might have a 300 horsepower engine, but those 300 horses are pulling a colossal weight – maybe as much as 100 tonnes. That's like saddling each horse with a 330 kg (730 lb) load, which is about the weight of 6 jockeys.

330 kg per horsepower ...or a bunch of jockies

35 seconds

CAMPER VAN

The VW camper – probably the nearest any van has got to being cool – has a modest 60 horsepower. It weighs about 2 tonnes, which means each "horse" only has to carry about 33 kg (73 lb): about the weight of a child. Mind you, the VW camper isn't very quick when there's a large family crammed inside.

33 kg per horsepower ... or a child

14 seconds

PORSCHE BOXSTER

The Boxster has has an impressive 260 horsepower engine, but it weighs 1.4 tonnes – comparable to the camper van. It's a lot faster, but it's far from being the swiftest or most nimble sports car, because it's weight holds it back.

5.4 kg per horsepower ... a small dog

6.4 seconds

ARIEL ATOM

The winner by a long way is the Ariel Atom, which weighs only half a tonne yet has a 300 horsepower engine. That means each horse only has to carry the weight of a rabbit. And that makes the Atom one of the fastest accelerating road cars in the world.

1.5 kg per horsepower ... a rabbit

2.7 seconds

45

Ariel Atom

Despite appearances, this car is fully finished. The Ariel Atom's designer wanted to build a car that had the bare minimum of bodywork, giving it a fantastic power-to-weight ratio for great acceleration, and putting all its lovely mechanical bits on view. You don't commute to work in the Atom. It's for country driving on sunny days and blasting around race tracks faster than a Ferrari.

Pushrod-operated shock absorbers at the front and back give the Atom the dynamic handling of a racecar.

Acceleration: 0–60 in 2.7 seconds
(similar to a Formula 1 car)

Weight: 456 kg (1005 lb)
(half the weight of a Mini)

Power: 300 horsepower
(more than twice the power of a Mini)

There's not much bodywork on an Atom, which saves weight and allows easy access for adjustments. Panels are made of a woven fibre composite that is strong and light.

A steel roll bar around the air intake protects the driver's head if the car overturns in an accident. The tubular steel chassis is very strong and also protects the occupants. Looks great, too.

The air intake mounted behind the driver draws in hundreds of litres of air every second to feed a supercharged Honda engine that can power the car to a zippy top speed of 155 mph (250 km/h).

Twin exhausts **Rear engine**

The Atom's four-cylinder engine is mounted behind the driver, as in a racing car. This is the view you'll have if you're on a race track with one.

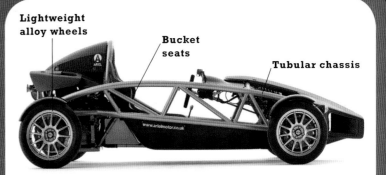

Lightweight alloy wheels **Bucket seats** **Tubular chassis**

One of the most unusual features of the Atom is its open frame construction. Made of lightweight stainless steel tubes, it is remarkably strong and safe. This car has no roof or windscreen, which makes helmets and weatherproof clothes essential at speed.

Inspired by NATURE

A car has to punch a hole through the air as it goes forward. As it speeds up, the air rushing past becomes a ferocious wind, holding the car back with a force known as **drag**. Drag robs energy from the car, slowing it down. So what's the solution? Answer: make the car as smooth and *streamlined* as possible – a trick that nature has been using for millions of years. The science of how shapes move in air is known as AERODYNAMICS.

This speedy fish has some style!

What's the best shape?

Hummer H1

Tall cars must punch a large hole through the air, which is hard work. The airstream collides with the sharp corners of the boxy shape, creating pockets of messy, swirling air – "turbulence" – over the bonnet and behind the car. Overcoming the force of drag and turbulence wastes energy and uses up the car's fuel.

Lamborghini Reventón

Smooth, long, and low cars push a small hole through the air. The disturbed air is able to flow more easily over the car's streamlined body, limiting the amount of drag and turbulence created. That means a higher top speed and better fuel efficiency.

This Corvette's mean look was inspired by the shape of a shark.

Changing shapes

Car designers have long tried to make cars streamlined, but in the beginning they did it purely by eye – and often got it wrong. Later, they started using wind tunnels and got better, turning aerodynamics into a science. In recent years, they discovered that streamlining is not the only thing that matters: really fast cars also need to create something called *downforce* to keep the wheels pushed down firmly on the ground.

Natural design

Some car designers take inspiration from the streamlined shapes of animals. The boxfish might seem a very unlikely starting point for a car, but nature has proved this shape to be perfectly streamlined. Designers at Mercedes-Benz copied the fish to create the highly fuel-efficient Bionic car, which does 70 miles (113 km) to the gallon.

The boxfish's shape was modelled on a computer and then adapted to form the car's body.

Wireframe computer model

Mercedes-Benz Bionic car

✳ In the 1930s, style was everything. This 1935 Mercedes-Benz had plenty of it. Unfortunately, the windscreen and flowing wings created loads of drag.

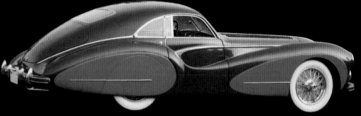

✳ This gorgeous 1948 Talbot Lago's shape was influenced by aeroplane design. And it wasn't just a pretty car: in 1950 it won the famous Le Mans 24-hour race.

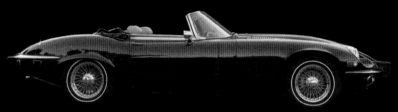

✳ The 1961 Jaguar E-Type's shape was the work of an aeroplane designer. It's very sleek, but the shape of the back creates lift, which can ruin grip.

✳ In 1969, Porsche built a racing car called the 917. It did 240 mph (386 km/h) but was very difficult to drive at high speed. Porsche put it in a wind tunnel and sorted out the aerodynamics by adding an upturned rear that pushed the wind upwards, creating downforce. It won Le Mans the next year.

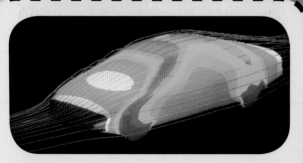

Airflow test

Designers of cars use computer programs that can simulate moving air. This allows a car's shape to be tested and moulded on screen before the car is built. The real car is tested in a large wind tunnel where a jet of air and smoke or white gas is blown over the car to reveal the shape of the airflow.

✳ Porsche was one of the first companies to use a wind tunnel, but today Formula 1 engineers seem to spend half their lives in wind tunnels, perfecting their cars' aerodynamics by making endless tiny adjustments.

The science of airflow

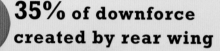

Because a **Formula 1 car** moves fast enough to take off like a plane, the greatest challenge it faces is keeping its wheels firmly on the ground. It does so by channelling the air in ways that push the car down, creating what scientists call **DOWNFORCE.**

The air intake above the driver's seat channels 300 litres of air into the engine every second – enough to keep 3000 people breathing.

35% of downforce created by rear wing

40% of downforce created under the car

Need for speed

Downforce is essential to keep a Formula 1 car under control. Unless the wheels are pressed firmly to the ground, their grip is poor and the car is in danger of skidding when it turns. But it's impossible to generate downforce without driving at speed. So to stay in control, the Formula 1 driver must go as fast as possible round every bend.

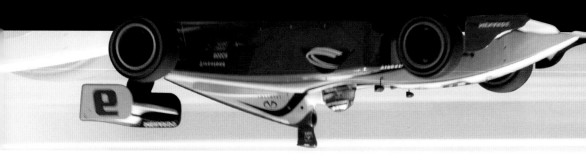

A plane uses wings to push itself up, but an F1 car uses wings to push itself *down*. The rear wing has the same curved "aerofoil" shape as a plane's wing, but it's upside down. As a result, it bends the airflow upwards, which – thanks to **Newton's third law** – creates an equal and opposite force pushing down: the downforce. Wind is also deliberately channelled under the car between a series of channels (the diffuser) that widen towards the rear, causing the air to speed up. Faster air has lower pressure, so the air rushing under the car creates suction, adding to the downforce.

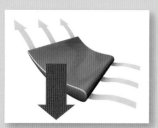

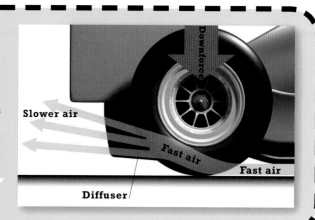

Slower air

Fast air

Fast air

Diffuser

25% of downforce from front wing

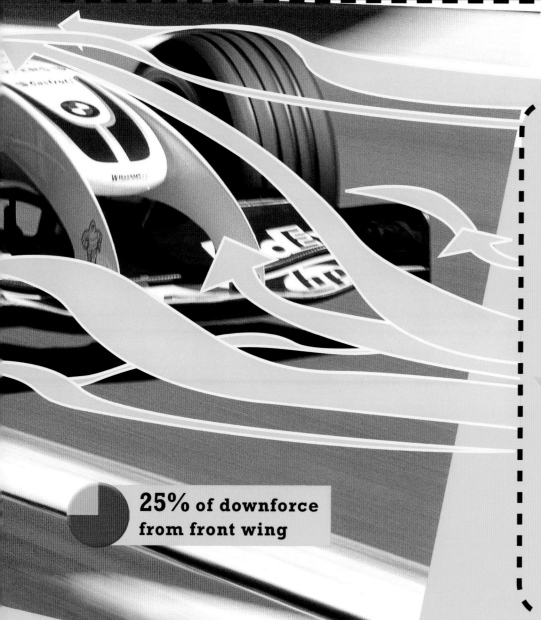

Ferocious air

As an F1 car nears its peak speed of around 225 mph (360 km/h), air flows over it with the force of a tornado.

The car must somehow push its way under this ferocious air stream and disturb it as little as possible. If the wind is stirred up into whirlpools – "vortices" – then these will rob the car of energy and slow it down.

So cars are designed to be as low and streamlined as possible. For the driver, the roaring winds are exhilarating but deadly: a careless manoeuvre that destabilizes the airflow could very quickly lead to loss of control and a crash.

Ouch!

1899

Belgian Camille Jenatzy became the first person to travel over 60 mph (96 km/h). Nicknamed the Red Devil, because of his ginger beard, he set the record three times in 1899 driving electric-powered cars.

1904

American car maker Henry Ford raised the record to 91 mph (146 km/h) racing on the frozen water of Lake St Clair. Co-driver Spider Huff crouched on the car's floor holding the accelerator down so Ford could concentrate on steering.

1906

No woman has ever held the land-speed record, but many have attempted it. England's Dorothy Levitt broke the women's speed record in 1903 when she notched up 96 mph (155 km/h) in this open-topped car.

60 mph : 96 km/h

91 mph : 146 km/h

96 mph : 155 km/h

Record breakers

In theory, there's only one limit to how fast a car can go: nothing in the universe can go beyond the speed of light (670 million mph or 1100 million km/h) – the ultimate speed limit. In practice, building a car that can go at even a millionth of this speed has proved remarkably hard.

Suppose you start with a standard car engine. You could add twice as many cylinders to burn twice as much fuel, but you wouldn't get twice the speed, because the pistons in an engine can pump only so fast. You could switch from a piston engine to an aeroplane jet engine – but then you'd hit aerodynamic limits instead. Above 200 mph (322 km/h), virtually all your fuel is being used to overcome drag. Unless your car is designed to force air upwards (and create downforce), there's every chance the jet engine will do what it's designed to do and you'll take off like a plane. Limitations like these set a practical limit to how fast cars can go – which is why breaking the land-speed record is one of the ultimate achievements.

1963

American drivers held the land-speed record almost continuously in the 20 years from 1963. Craig Breedlove's three-wheeled *Spirit of America*, which reached 408 mph (657 km/h), was the first of a series of frighteningly fast cars based on turbojet aeroplane engines.

1965

American grain farmer Art Arfons snatched the speed record three times in quirky cars nicknamed *The Green Monster*, hand-built from junkyard parts. A tyre blew out at 600 mph (966 km/h) during his record attempt on 7 November 1965, but Arfon still stopped safely.

1970

A year after rocket power took astronauts to the Moon, a rocket car blasted American Gary Gabelich to a new land-speed record of 622 mph (1001 km/h). Gabelich was planning for a new record of 800 mph (1287 km/h) when he was killed in a motorcycle accident in 1984.

408 mph : 657 km/h

600 mph : 966 km/h

622 mph : 1001 km/h

1924

In 1924, English speed king Sir Malcolm Campbell achieved 146 mph (235 km/h). He went on to break this record a further eight times in a series of famous cars named *Blue Bird*. In 1935 he finally succeeded in going faster than 300 mph (483 km/h).

> **146 mph : 235 km/h**

1929

Henry Segrave's *Golden Arrow* used technical improvements to snatch a new record of 231 mph (372 km/h). Engineered to produce downforce, it was packed with ice to stop it overheating, and was steered like a bullet using a telescopic rifle sight.

> **231 mph : 372 km/h**

1947

Conventional cars were too slow to push the record any further. When John Cobb set new records in 1938 and 1939, he used two supercharged aeroplane engines in his turtle-shaped Railton Mobil Special. He achieved speeds of 368 mph (592 km/h) and 394 mph (634 km/h).

> **400 mph : 644 km/h**

Jet power

You can go much faster with a jet engine behind you. Jet engines don't have pistons pushing cylinders up and down. They suck in air at the front, use it to burn fuel, and blast out hot exhaust gases. The backward-moving gas rockets you forward, just like Newton predicted.

> It's the Law!
> (My 3rd one)

Getting faster!

	Electric cars
	Steam cars
	Petrol cars
	Jet and rocket cars

(Chart: Speed vs Year. Speed axis: 100 mph (160 km/h), 200 mph (322 km/h), 300 mph (483 km/h), 400 mph (644 km/h), 500 mph (805 km/h), 600 mph (966 km/h), 700 mph (1126 km/h), 800 mph (1287 km/h). Year axis: 1880, 1900, 1920, 1940, 1960, 1980, 2000, 2020.)

Land-speed-record drivers get lots of help from engineers who push car technology to the limit. The first records were set around 1900 by electric cars. Switching to steam and petrol power pushed the record to new heights until the limits of petrol power were reached in the 1940s. In the 1960s, American engineers increased the record by more than 50% by switching to jet and rocket engines. The last two records have been broken by cars using jet-fighter engines.

The North American Eagle (left) is currently under development. Engineers hope its turbojet engine will power it to a record-breaking 800 mph (1287 km/h).

1983

Europeans recaptured the speed record in 1983 when Englishman Richard Noble raced to 633 mph (1019 km/h) in *Thrust 2*. Built around an enormous Rolls-Royce jet engine, it weighed almost four tonnes – several times heavier than a typical family car.

> **633 mph : 1019 km/h**

1997

The land-speed record is currently held by *Thrust SSC*, also developed by Richard Noble. It became the world's first supersonic (faster-than-sound) car when British fighter pilot Andy Green drove it to 766 mph (1233 km/h) in October 1997.

> **766 mph : 1233 km/h**

Monday morning: *invent car.* **Monday lunchtime:** *try to make car faster.* That's right, as soon as the car was invented we started trying to make it faster. Trouble is, there's more to driving than speed and power. A car needs to be able to *apply* all that lovely power in just the right way, otherwise you might as well use it to boil a kettle. And that brings us to a word you'll read all the time in car magazines: handling.

Handling is all to do with making a car go along the road without sliding off into a field. Sliding off into fields wastes time, is rather dangerous, and upsets cows.

To make a car handle well we need to get to grips with tyres, suspension, weight, and we need to unravel the mysteries of understeer and oversteer (which are types of skid). And when you understand all these things and their relationship with science, you'll be a better driver. And on a racing circuit a quicker one.

Handling

Science *friction*

Nothing's quite as smooth as it seems. The surface of any object is covered in microscopic lumps and bumps that snag against anything they touch. The result is a force that stops things moving freely, and we call that force *friction*. Friction affects cars in dozens of different ways, but is it your friend or your foe?

Friction helps things stick, improves your grip, and keeps you in control.

FRIEND

Tyres

Friction helps tyres bite the tarmac. Without it, a car's wheels would just slip and spin – and it would go nowhere. Tyres are one of the most important parts of the car. Often tyres are specially designed for a particular car or different weather conditions.

Pedals

Your feet need a good grip on the pedals to drive safely. Pedals either have rubber pads fitted to them or have grooves cut into them to provide a rough surface that stops your foot sliding off. The grooves look much cooler – and that's what racing cars have.

Grip

Look closely at your fingertips: they are covered with ridges a bit like the treads of tyres. Dozens of these grooves on each finger improve grip by increasing the *static friction* between your hands and the steering wheel.

Brakes

Car brakes bring you to a halt by pressing pads made from a tough material against the surface of a disc inside the wheels until they stop turning. This massive dose of *sliding friction* turns the kinetic energy of the car into heat. Formula 1 cars use carbon fibre discs because they're light and very tough.

Hot stuff

When you step on the brakes, friction helps you stop by converting your kinetic energy into heat. In Formula 1 cars, the brake pads create so much friction that they can heat to more than 500°C (1000°F) and glow bright yellow. This thermal photograph shows how hot an ordinary car's wheels get when it brakes. The front wheels get much hotter than the back ones because the car's weight shifts to the front as you decelerate.

Two types of friction

STATIC friction

Friction between the tyres and the road stops a parked car from sliding down a hill when the handbrake is on. This kind of **GRIP** between two stationary surfaces is called static friction. A bit like invisible glue, it's very powerful. Static friction is what stops wheels spinning or sliding sideways as cars go round bends.

SLIDING friction

Try and drag a heavy box across the floor. At first it won't budge, because static friction is holding it back. But once it **SLIPS**, the job is easy, because now a much *weaker kind of friction* is at work: sliding friction. When cars skid on wet roads, tyres lose the force of static friction, and sliding friction takes over.

or FOE?

Friction wears out your engine and slows you down at high speeds.

Seat

Friction between your clothes and the seat stops you sliding around while you are in the car. Fabric-covered seats have a rougher surface, which gives a better grip than shiny leather or plastic seats.

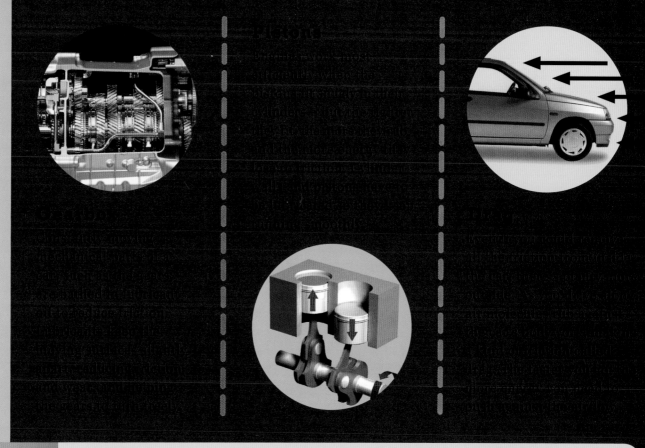

Fighting friction

If friction is the enemy of moving parts, lubrication (oiling things) is the enemy of friction. Liquids like oil make good lubricants because they spread between touching surfaces and can move about, preventing the tiny bumps and lumps from snagging. Bearings (rolling balls sandwiched between two moving metal parts) are another way of reducing friction.

Black magic

FOOTPRINT, ACTUAL SIZE

Tyres are what actually push a car along, and they do it by applying the force of friction.

They do this in a surprisingly ingenious way. To give the car maximum push, tyres must grip the ground with the powerful force of "static friction". But how can a moving tyre possibly have static friction? Easy: because the wheel is rolling, the point of contact with the road is actually always still (and the top of the tyre is moving twice as fast as the car).

As well as maximizing static friction, tyres must *minimize* another kind of friction, called rolling resistance. Rolling resistance happens because tyres are repeatedly squeezed underneath (where wheels press on them) and stretched at the top (when wheels release them). All that stretching and squeezing wastes energy you could be using to go forwards.

Gaining ground

It's easy to see how Newton's third law makes a rocket fly when it blasts hot gas backwards. What's less obvious is that tyres work the same way. When wheels turn, tyres push back against the road – and so the road pushes you forwards. The action (tyres pushing backwards) gives an equal and opposite reaction (car going forwards).

Tyre pushes backwards

Wheel moves forwards

The pushing force from a tyre doesn't just make the car roll forwards – it actually makes planet Earth roll backwards, but only by a tiny, tiny, tiny, tiny bit. If Earth were much lighter than your car, the car would stay almost still and Earth would roll by underneath – a bit like a hamster wheel.

Footprints

This is the life-size footprint of a person's shoe. To the right is the "footprint" of a typical car tyre, also life-size. The whole tyre may look big, but the area of contact with the ground is no greater than that of a man's foot. Only four tiny "contact patches" like this hold a car to the road, yet they have to move and manoeuvre a vehicle that weighs 20 times more than a man and moves ten times faster.

You go one way, Earth goes the other

Tyre contact with road

TYRE FOOTPRINT, ACTUAL SIZE

Tyre teamwork

Different bits of the tyre tread work as a team to keep you on the road. The blocks and ribs in the middle form the major part of the tyre's gripping surface, while the sipes make the tyre bend more to improve handling. The shoulders add grip when you're cornering. The grooves are the drains: the tyre squeezes water along them as it presses the road and pushes it out to the side.

Grooves **Ribs**

Blocks **Dimples**

Sipes **Shoulder**

The tweel

Tyres are pumped with air because, apart from gripping, another important job they have to do is cushion bumps – they help the suspension. Instead of an air cushion, a tweel (a wheel crossed with a tyre) has flexible polyurethane spokes that bend and spring back to shape. Because there's no air inside, tweels make punctures a thing of the past.

At 60 mph (100 km/h) on a wet road, the grooves on a tyre can pump out 2 gallons (7.5 litres) of water every second.

Different tyres for different jobs

ALL-terrain vehicle

Deserts, rivers, rocks, and mud – nothing stops a HMMWV (High Mobility Multipurpose Wheeled Vehicle, pronounced "humvee" or Hummer for short). Designed for military use over rough terrain, civilians can now buy smaller versions of the original aircraft-carrier-sized humvee. All Hummers have a low centre of gravity, a powerful engine, and some clever technology help them stay the right way up.

The Hummer was built for power and off-road agility. A V8 engine produces three times the horsepower of a family car, giving it superb climbing and scrambling ability.

Powerful gas-filled shock absorbers allow the wheels to rise and fall independently over bumps. Even if several wheels are stuck in mud or spinning in mid-air, the Hummer can still get itself out of trouble. It uses differential gears to redirect the engine torque away from the wheels that are stuck, feeding more to the wheels that can still grip – and so powers itself free.

The Hummer's self-levelling suspension system allows its wheels to tilt on bumpy ground while the body remains level.

Stability The centre of gravity is the point inside an object where all its weight seems to be concentrated. Like anything else, cars tend to topple over if their centre of gravity is too high or moves too much to one side. A Hummer is longer than a typical 4x4, with the wheels nearer the front and back, and it has a heavy, low engine. This squat design gives it a very low centre of gravity. It can drive up, down, or sideways on slopes as long as its centre of gravity stays inside the lines of stability (where its tyres meet the ground).

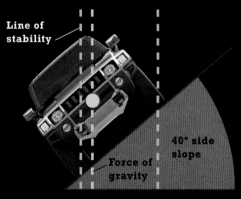

Line of stability

Force of gravity

40° side slope

Stable

Driving a Hummer on a 40° slope is easy. The car's massive, 3-tonne weight acts down through the centre of gravity, and since this is safely between the two lines of stability, there is no risk of toppling. The tyres don't slip, thanks to chunky treads up to 13 mm (0.5 in) deep – at least 50 per cent deeper than normal tyres.

⬤ = car's centre of gravity

No surface is too much for this all-action vehicle

Properly pumped-up tyres help a car go quickly, safely, and save fuel. But in off-road mud, flatter, squashier tyres give more grip and better handling. In a Hummer, the driver can pump the tyres up or down automatically, to suit different terrain, using a switch on the dashboard.

With their engine air intakes high up the bonnet, Hummers can easily drive through shallow rivers. Military Hummers come with a snorkel that feeds air into the engine in water up to 1.5 m (5 ft) deep.

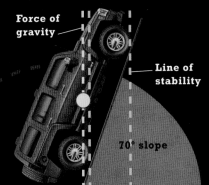

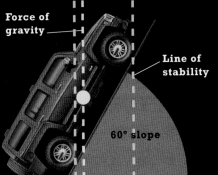

Force of gravity

Line of stability

60° slope

Stable

Driving forwards, the Hummer can tackle slope angles up to 60°. With a heavy 6.2-litre engine at the front, the centre of gravity lies safely towards the front of the car and within the lines of stability. Most 4x4 cars struggle to climb slopes steeper than 45°.

Force of gravity

Line of stability

Roll over

70° slope

Unstable

On a slightly steeper slope, the centre of gravity is no longer between the lines of stability. Gravity will tend to tip the car backwards, causing the car to roll.

MONSTER TRUCKS

Monster trucks regularly perform freestyle stunts, including wheelies, jumping, ...

Take a four-wheel-drive truck, beef up the engine, gearbox, and tyres, reinforce the chassis, and add a sprinkling of science – and you get a monster truck: the sort of car that can **really** make a lasting impression.

This monster truck, Bigfoot, has tyres 170 cm (66 in) in diameter and 110 cm (43 in) wide. By spreading the truck's 4.5 tonne weight over a bigger area, huge tyres reduce pressure on the ground, so the wheels can speed through thick mud.

... and car crushing.

Even though Bigfoot is three times heavier than a normal car, its supercharged, methanol-powered engine gives it a top speed of 70 mph (112 km/h). Driving up a ramp, it can use its momentum to clear 14 parked cars. One truck, Bigfoot 14, has even managed to jump over a Boeing 727 airliner.

Monster trucks get their amazing ability to climb cars and leap obstacles from their suspension. Massive tyres, gigantic springs, and efficient shock absorbers all contribute to the suspension system. The same three parts are at work in all cars. Suspension systems act to keep the body of the car level when going over bumps by damping the vertical motion of the wheels.

Tyres

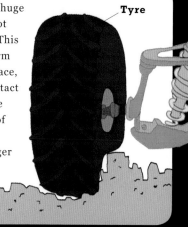

Tyre

Despite their huge size, Bigfoot's tyres are not pumped to full pressure. This allows the rubber to deform around bumps in the surface, increasing the area in contact with the ground. Since the tyres support the weight of the truck, spreading the force of impact over a larger area makes the tyre less likely to burst when landing.

Spring

Spring

When a wheel hits a bump, the sturdy metal spring stretches or squeezes as the wheel moves up or down. Unless it is damped, the spring will keep bouncing up and down, because there's nowhere for the energy to go.

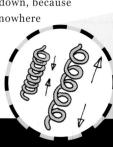

Shock absorber

Shock absorber

A shock absorber, or damper, is a pump filled with gas that absorbs energy from the spring and transfers it to a piston. The piston pushes against the gas, which slows the piston down and turns its energy into heat.

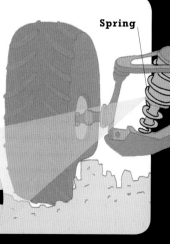

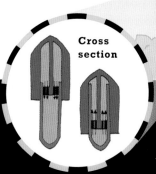

Cross section

Shock absorbers are speed sensitive – the faster the suspension moves, the more resistance the damper provides.

63

Keep on moving ...

The science of inertia

Isaac Newton discovered a very important law about moving objects. He realized that once an object is moving, it likes to keep on moving in a straight line at a constant speed. And if it's not moving, it likes to stay still. This stubbornness has a scientific name: INERTIA. It's inertia that makes snooker balls roll in straight lines, and it's inertia that makes shopping trolleys such a pain to steer, especially when they're full.

> I always wear a seatbelt because my first law of motion says I have to. If I didn't, inertia might send me hurtling through the windscreen if my car suddenly stopped. Which might hurt. A lot.

It's the law! (Newton's first one)

There's something odd about Newton's first law. Newton said that moving objects will carry on in a straight line forever unless a force stops them, but common sense tells us that moving objects usually grind to a halt. That's because there usually *is* a force trying to stop them: the force of friction. Take away that (by going into space, for instance), and Newton's first law works rather well. In fact, it keeps all the stars, planets, and moons moving.

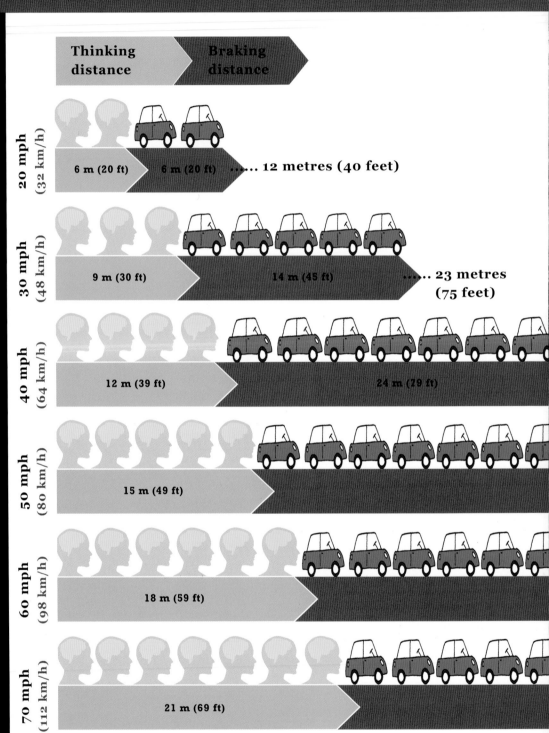

Stopping distance

To stop a moving car, you have to overcome its inertia by using a force: friction from the brakes. The brakes get rid of the car's kinetic energy by turning it into heat energy and sound, but they are designed to do this gradually – otherwise the car would stop in an instant and *your* inertia would send you flying out of your seat. The faster a car is going, the more kinetic energy it has, and the longer the brakes take to stop it. The chart shows how far a car's inertia will carry it when a driver stops in an emergency. The total stopping distance has two parts: thinking distance (when the driver is reacting) and braking distance (when the driver has slammed his foot on the brakes).

Why are cars such an effort to stop and start?

There's no escaping inertia ...

The only way to overcome inertia is to apply a force. You need a massive force to overcome the inertia of a standing car. But once the car's moving, inertia makes it easier to push.

You have to overcome inertia to make a car turn, otherwise it will keep going in a straight line. Tyres use the force of friction to overcome inertia, but the passengers' inertia pushes them the other way.

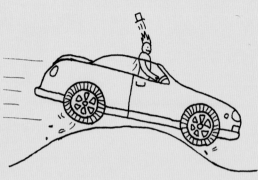

Ever flown into the air when your car went over a bump? It was inertia that kept you and your car floating in the air for a moment before the force of gravity pulled you down.

As a car's speed rises, the braking distance leaps up by bigger and bigger increments. The world's fastest car – Thrust SSC – has a total stopping distance of 6 miles (10 km).

36 metres (118 feet)

38 m (125 ft)

53 metres (175 feet)

55 m (180 ft)

73 metres (240 feet)

75 m (246 ft)

96 metres (315 feet)

Thinking time

Drivers need lightning reactions to stay safe in an emergency. Most drivers take 0.7 seconds to respond to a sudden hazard, but this thinking time can more than treble if a person has consumed alcohol or if they're distracted by a mobile phone. And that can add hundreds of feet to the stopping distance, making an accident far more likely.

Keep your head on

A Formula 1 driver's body fits snugly inside his car, but his head pokes out of the top of the cabin, and his heavy helmet adds to his head's inertia. In a high-speed crash, head + helmet try to keep moving forward after the car has stopped, straining the driver's neck as though his head weighed half a tonne. This is not good for his neck. So as a precaution, Formula 1 drivers now bolt their heads to the car using a special "head and neck support system" (HANS).

G-force

Imagine you're a Formula 1 driver. As your car hurtles round the track, accelerating and decelerating suddenly, and twisting violently around the bends, tremendous forces seem to be shoving your body back and forth or from side to side. This shoving is caused by inertia: your body is trying to obey Newton's first law and keep going in straight line at a constant speed, but the car won't let it. The result is a powerful force that feels like gravity acting in strange directions – like gravity gone mad. We call it **G-force.**

3 G Acceleration

A Formula 1 car can accelerate from 0 to 60 mph (0–96 km/h) in less than two seconds. This phenomenal acceleration generates a G-force in the opposite direction and presses the driver into the back of his seat with a force three times his body weight.

G-force

5 G Downforce

When the car hits top speed along the straights, aerodynamic effects create up to 5 G of downforce, ramming the car's tyres down onto the road. But this isn't the same as G-force, and the driver feels no downward force on his body.

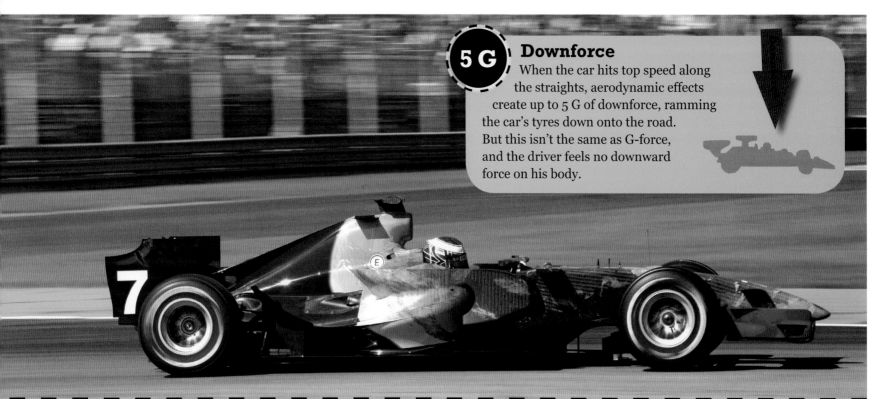

What's the maximum G-force a person can take? That's the question that the brave (or mad) scientist John Stapp tried to answer in 1954 when he strapped himself into an insanely dangerous rocket-powered train sled and then decelerated from 630 mph (1017 km/h) to zero in 1.25 seconds, generating 46 G. He briefly weighed 3 tonnes and his eyes filled with blood – but he survived.

4 G Cornering

In the bends, inertia tries to make the driver go in a straight line, so he feels a G-force pushing him outwards with up to four times his weight. The bucket-seat holds him tight, but he must strain against the force to keep his head straight and his hands on the steering wheel.

G-force

6 G Braking

The carbon brakes used in Formula 1 are unbelievably powerful. They cause such violent deceleration that the driver is thrust forwards by 6 G – as much G-force as a fighter pilot must endure. The force squeezes tears from the driver's eyes and splatters his visor.

G-force

G-force limits

–3 G

The maximum negative G-force a person can take. Negative Gs push blood up into the brain and can burst blood vessels

Zero G

Weightlessness in space

1 G

Normal gravity

3 G

The maximum G-force experienced at the bottom of a hill on a big rollercoaster

4.3 G

The maximum G-force that civilian aircraft are built to withstand

5 G

The point at which most people black out if G-force is sustained

5.1 G

The G-force generated by top dragsters during maximum acceleration

9 G

The maximum G-force that fighter pilots are trained to withstand during aerial manoeuvres

46 G

The maximum G-force deliberately endured by a human being

100 G

Exposure to 100 G is almost always fatal, however brief

180 G

The maximum G-force a human being has survived

In the HOT seat

What's it like to drive a Formula 1 car? Extremely difficult. What's it like to compete in a Formula 1 race? Almost impossible. F1 cars are blindingly fast and incredibly sensitive to the driver's controls, which makes lightning reactions and supreme concentration essential. Yet the driver must battle continually with violent G-forces, sweltering heat, and deafening noise – all of which makes competing in Formula 1 as physically exhausting as running a marathon.

Mental training is just as important for F1 drivers as physical – no other sport demands such intense concentration. Drivers train with psychologists to ensure they have unwavering mind control during the race. They memorize maps and visualize the perfect lap, so that when they arrive at the track they feel like they've driven it many times before.

THE STEERING WHEEL gives the driver control of everything except acceleration and braking, so he need never take his hands off. Gears are changed by flappy paddles, and the small buttons control a host of functions (many kept secret) from traction control to a drinks dispenser – drinks are pumped by tube straight to the driver's mouth.

Ferrari 2008 steering wheel

IN THE COCKPIT

Drivers sit so close to the ground that they sometimes get heat blisters on their backside. The car has very little suspension, which means drivers feel every bump in the road – and painfully. Knee and ankle protectors can help prevent the inevitable bruises caused by violent jolts to the car.

OUCH!

F1 cars have tailor-made "bucket seats" moulded to a cast of the driver's body. The seat must hold the driver snugly to prevent G-force throwing him sideways. A tough six-part harness keeps the driver tightly strapped in. Without this, he'd be thrown from the car when braking suddenly.

Harness

The driver's suit amounts to a high-tech suit of armour. Its most important job is to protect him from fire in case the car crashes and the fuel tank is ruptured. Almost every part of the driver's body is covered by a fireproof fabric called Nomex.

Perfect physical fitness is essential to withstand the intense ordeal of F1 racing. Drivers are said to have the most finely tuned bodies on Earth – fitter than football players and leaner than athletes.

A BALACLAVA
made of Nomex protects the head from intense heat. Only eyes and nose remain uncovered – for vision and breathing.

THE HEAD AND NECK are the
only parts of the body that are not well supported. G-force multiplies the effective weight of head and helmet to 30 kg (66 lb) during intense braking and cornering, straining the neck. Drivers must build up neck muscles with special exercises so they can take the strain.

THE HELMET must pass
a battery of strict safety tests:

A pointed 3-kg (7-lb) metal weight dropped from 3 metres (10 ft) high must not pierce the helmet's tough shell.

The temperature inside must not exceed 70ºC (158ºF) when the helmet is blasted with 800ºC (1500ºF) flames for 45 seconds.

The chinstrap must be able to support a 38 kg (84 lb) weight without stretching more than 30 mm (1.2 in).

HEART RATE
soars to 200 beats per minute as a driver approaches difficult turns. At rest, F1 drivers have a pulse of under 60.

THE SPINE
is subjected to up to 3 G of compression force during braking. Cockpit vibrations also put massive strain on the bones of the spine, the back muscles, and on spinal nerves – potentially causing long-term damage.

UP TO 3G

OVERALLS are made of 2–4
layers of Nomex. Gloves consist of a double layer of Nomex with a reinforcing layer of leather on the inside. The gloves must provide protection while also allowing free movement of hands and fingers for operating the controls.

THE HEAT is almost unbearable during a F1
race. The driver might as well be sitting in an oven: the tyres reach boiling point, brakes become yellow-hot, and the roaring engine is right behind him. To make things worse, his body is trapped in a tight space and cocooned in many layers of stifling fireproofed clothing. Cockpit temperatures can reach 60ºC (140ºF), and the driver can lose 3 kg (7 lb) of his weight in sweat due to heat and physical exertion.

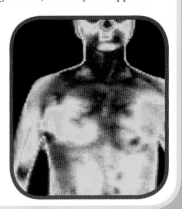

NOMEX SHOES
must protect the feet without impairing touch, which is vital for control of the car's only two pedals (accelerator and brake). A thin rubber sole provides excellent grip.

Wall of death

In the circus stunt known as the **"wall of death"**, motorbikes and even cars ride around a nearly vertical wall, seeming to defy the law of gravity. What's keeping them up? The answer is CENTRIFUGAL FORCE (which is really just another name for the G-force caused by inertia) and FRICTION. Any object that travels in a circle will feel centrifugal force pushing it outwards. Washing machines use centrifugal force to drive water out of clothes during the spin cycle, and fairground rides use it to make you feel sick.

The faster an object hurtles round, the more powerful the force. To stay on the wall of death, the car has to go fast enough for centrifugal force to push its tyres firmly against the wall – only then will the tyres create enough friction to grip the surface and resist the pull of gravity. If the car slows down, gravity wins out and the car will tumble off and smash to the ground. At this wall of death in India, it looks like a few planks have been pinched by spectators – which could have rather unfortunate consequences.

FRICTION vs INERTIA:
The science of skids

A car's tyres fight a never-ending battle against its inertia. Cars want to move in straight lines at constant speed (thank Newton's first law), but the tyres must use the force of friction to grip the road and push the car around bends, overcoming inertia. Most of the time they win the battle, but sometimes they lose. And when that happens, tyres lose their grip and slide screeching across the tarmac – the car has gone into a ***skid***. Skids are involved in a quarter of all crashes, so knowing how to regain control is a matter of life and death.

FRONT-WHEEL SKID (UNDERSTEER)

Help! I can't turn sharply enough!

What happens: Front wheels lose grip and the car fails to turn as sharply as it should.
Cause: Driving too fast while turning or braking too hard while turning.
Remedy: Remove the cause by taking your foot off the accelerator or brake pedal. If possible, straighten the steering momentarily.

What happens: Rear wheels lose their grip, causing the back of the car to swing round.
Cause: Accelerating round a corner or sudden braking in a rear-wheel-drive car.
Remedy: Remove the cause by taking your foot off the accelerator or brake and turning the steering wheel the opposite way.

REAR-WHEEL SKID (OVERSTEER)

*Now I'm turning **too** sharply!!!*

What causes skids?

Skids happen when the force of friction under the tyres is overcome by a more powerful force. A sharp turn, sudden acceleration or heavy braking can all induce forces powerful enough to overcome grip. If the road is wet or icy, friction is much weaker and skids are far more likely to happen. On very wet roads, a wedge of water can build up in front of the tyre and then lift it slightly off the road, causing the car to skate uncontrollably. This is called aquaplaning.

Normal   **Aquaplaning**

FOUR-WHEEL SKID

Now I'm not turning at all! Aaarrgghh!!

What happens: All four wheels lose grip, causing the car to slide in a straight line like a shopping trolley.
Cause: Sudden braking in wet or icy conditions.
Remedy: Press the brakes firmly, but if the wheels lock up, momentarily release the brakes and press again.

Regaining control of a skidding car can be a bit hairy, not to mention dangerous. So a better strategy is to avoid skidding in the first place. Modern cars now come equipped with cunning gadgets that can detect the first sign of a skid by monitoring the wheels. If some wheels start spinning much faster or slower than others, they've lost grip and could cause a skid.

Traction control systems use sensors to monitor the turning speed of the wheels. If one of the driven wheels (the ones that the engine is driving) is turning much faster than the others, it must have lost grip. The traction control computer spots this and either cuts the engine power briefly, applies the brakes, or both.

Anti-lock braking systems (ABS) come into play if a wheel stops turning – a sign that the brake has "locked" the wheel, which can happen on wet or icy roads. The system automatically releases and re-applies the brake in short bursts, allowing the wheel to roll and so regain its grip of the road.

Brake

Electronic stability program (ESP) uses information from sensors to detect when the car is about to skid and then applies braking force to one or more wheels to correct it, while also reducing engine power. It's a brilliant safety system and all cars should have it. Within a few years they will.

Losing your grip

Skids can be pretty scary when they catch you unawares. For a second or two, you lose control of the car and may find yourself watching helplessly as you career gracefully off the road in a completely unexpected direction, wondering where you might end up. So it might come as a surprise to learn that skilled drivers often induce skids deliberately – sometimes just for the thrill of it, and sometimes to enable tricky manoeuvres. Here are a few tricks of the trade. Oh, and **DON'T** try these at home.

POWERSLIDING

A powerslide is a deliberate rear-wheel skid. The easiest way to do it is to step hard on the accelerator in a rear-wheel drive car while turning sharply. The sudden burst of power at the rear wheels causes them to spin and lose grip in the turn, with the result that the back of the car swings out sideways rather than following the front into the turn. The driver then turns the steering wheel into the skid so that the car slides sideways, with the rear wheels still skidding and the front wheels rolling. There are several other ways of inducing powerslides, but all of them work the same way, causing loss of traction at the rear.

HANDBRAKE TURN

By using the handbrake to lock the rear wheels and so destroy their grip, a driver can swing a car through 180° in a tight space and shoot off in the opposite direction. Handy for chases.

DOUGHNUT

The idea here is simply to spin a car round and round wildly with the wheels at one or both ends skidding. If the tyres screech, smoke, and make a doughnut pattern of skid marks, so much the better. Ideal for causing injuries, noise and damage to cars or property. Not much use otherwise, though some racing drivers entertain fans with victory doughnuts after winning races.

BURNOUT

This means spinning the rear wheels while a car is standing or moving slowly, and it usually involves a lot of noise and smoke. Handy in drag racing, where it provides a quick means of heating the tyres, which in turn provides maximum grip.

FISHTAILING

Fishtailing happens by accident when rear-wheel drive cars lose grip at the rear in a turn and swing round. The driver tries to correct the skid with steering but overdoes it, causing the tail to flick the other way (like a fish). If the driver fails to regain control, the swings get worse until the car spins out of control.

J-TURN

This is a bit like a handbrake turn, except that the car starts off reversing rapidly and then swings through a tight half-turn to point forward, before racing away. Perfect for a rapid getaway, and often seen done by stunt-drivers in films. Although it looks and sounds more exciting if the tyres squeal and burn, no skidding is needed – just quick reactions and good control. Think of it as a turbo-charged version of reverse parking.

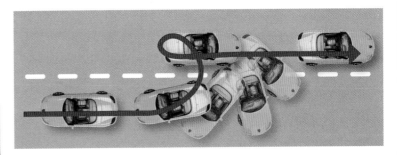

PIT manoeuvre

How do you stop a speeding car? US police departments use the Pursuit Intervention Technique. The police driver drives beside the car being pursued but holds back slightly to align the front of his car with the rear of the suspect's car. Then he turns sharply to ram the side of the suspect's car and make its rear wheels break from the road and lose grip, causing a fishtail.

When a car hits another object at speed, something has to give. Cars can be designed to survive crashes without a scratch – but **we need to survive** them, too.

It takes forces to make things move and forces to stop them. To stop something gradually and gently, a small force is enough – think of the light touch on the brakes that can gradually slow a bike down. But to stop something very suddenly, you need a much larger force.

You can make a car accelerate from 0–60 mph (0–100km/h) in 5–10 seconds. But in a car crash, you can go from 60–0 in less than a second. You feel massive force when a car speeds up. You might feel 100 times more force when you crash because the deceleration happens so quickly.

Triple whammy

If you could study a car crash in slow-motion, you'd discover that there are actually three separate impacts (right). Each impact involves sudden deceleration, and that creates deadly forces. The secret to making cars safe is to *slow down* each impact, which prolongs the deceleration and therefore reduces the forces. Slowing down the impact by a fraction of a second can be enough to save lives.

1st impact
Car hits obstacle

2nd impact
Body hits inside of car (or would do if there wasn't an airbag)

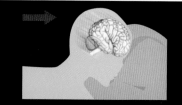

3rd impact
Brain hits skull (and may re-bound to hit back of skull too)

Crumple zones

At the front and rear of a car are "crumple zones" – areas deliberately designed to crumple up like a concertina in a collision. This slows down the car's deceleration and thereby dramatically reduces the impact forces. Just 1 m (3 ft) of crumpled car can cut the forces reaching the passengers by 90 per cent.

crasH

Built like us...

Head
Contains three force sensors to measure impacts on brain.

Neck
Has nine sensors and pulleys inside so it can move in any direction to measure whiplash.

Chest
Rib sensors measure impacts from seat belts or the steering wheel column.

Legs
Force sensors in the pelvis, thigh, knee, and ankles assess likelihood of fractures and dislocations of joints.

Skin
Steel and aluminium structure is covered with foam and vinyl to simulate skin puncture impacts.

Crash test dummies

They don't call them dummies for nothing. Well, would you sit in a car that was just about to crash? Once, engineers used dead bodies to test cars. Now they use plastic people, costing over £100,000, instead. They might look silly, but they're pretty smart inside. They're packed with 130 different sensors – concentrated in the head, chest, and upper leg (the bits most likely to get hurt). The bodies are weighted and jointed like real bodies: in a crash, the arms flail about and the head swings violently forward, just like the real thing. With computers recording everything the dummies feel, engineers know exactly what injuries people could get – and how to avoid them.

Believe it or not, some car colours appear to be much safer than others. A study in New Zealand in the late 90s found that you're more likely to have a crash if you drive a brown car rather than a silver one. But is this because silver cars are safer or because safe drivers prefer the colour silver? Or can they just be seen more easily?

The passenger safety cage is a rigid steel cell between the front and back crumple zones. Designed to stay the same shape even in a severe crash or rollover, it stops passengers getting squashed or trapped as the car changes shape. Impact energy is safely deflected around the passengers by the cage bars.

Airbags let the passengers stop more slowly than the car. When the airbag sensor detects a large deceleration (a sudden stop), the bags inflate in less than a twentieth of a second, giving a much softer impact than the steering wheel. Stopping the passenger more slowly means less force – and less damage.

Help! This is going to hurt

Seatbelts improve your chance of surviving a crash by 50–75 per cent, mainly by preventing inertia from throwing you through the windscreen. They also spread the force of impact over a larger area of your body, making injuries less severe. They stretch too, slowing you down more slowly so your body feels less force.

Size matters – when a car hits a truck, you're less likely to be injured if you're in the truck. It has more mass and energy, so it's harder to stop because its momentum continues to carry it forwards. As it thumps the car, it transfers a huge amount of energy – and that's what does the damage.

The petrol engine has ruled the world of cars for more than a century, but things may be about to change. Scientists and engineers are working flat out to come up with new technologies that do less harm to the environment, and the ideas they're working on will lead to some fantastic new cars. It's very exciting stuff.

Remember the first electric cars from the 1860s? They weren't very good because their batteries were heavy and went flat quickly. Well, the electric cars heading our way not only have much better batteries but deliver supercar performance, while also being as quiet as a mouse and a joy to drive. And there's loads more in the pipeline, from flying cars to cars that go underwater – so turn the page for a glimpse into the future.

Technology

What's it MADE of ?

Animal, vegetable, and mineral

A car is composed of elements from each of the three classifications – animal, vegetable, and mineral. The metals, originating in the last of the trio, provide by far the greatest overall contribution to a typical steel-bodied car.

0.5% cow

Leather is used for the seating and interior trim in some cars.

+

5% tree

Trees provide rubber for tyres and wood for steering wheels and trim.

Steel and aluminium

A steel chassis is usually made from a number of pressings that are then welded together. If you make the parts from aluminium instead, you halve their weight. Every piece of aluminium used to lighten a car cuts fuel consumption – over the lifetime of the vehicle, this saves at least **20 times** its weight in carbon dioxide emissions from entering the atmosphere.

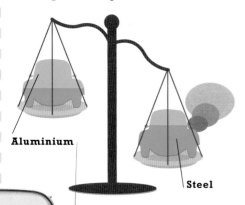

Aluminium

Steel

Kevlar When a car brakes, its pads create so much friction that they can heat to over 500°C (932°F)! Modern brake pads are made from heatproof materials including metals, ceramics, and composites based on Kevlar – carbon fibres knitted into fabric. Kevlar is five times stronger than steel and is also used to make bulletproof vests.

Carbon fibre and plastic

This Porsche incorporates carbon-fibre-reinforced plastic for its body parts, instead of steel or aluminium. The plastic body is moulded in a single piece to create a monocoque design. This makes the car especially rigid and strong.

Alloys If you run a car engine at moderate speed for an hour a day, the pistons will pump up and down **75 million** times in a year. Pistons are usually cast from strong, light, aluminium-silicon alloys. The silicon stops the aluminium from expanding as much, so the piston fits better at a wider range of temperatures. The fuel burns more cleanly in the cylinders, and so, the engine creates less pollution.

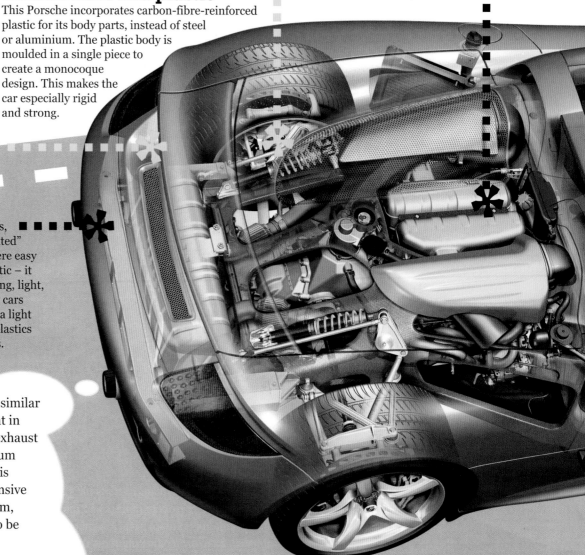

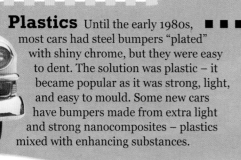

Plastics Until the early 1980s, most cars had steel bumpers "plated" with shiny chrome, but they were easy to dent. The solution was plastic – it became popular as it was strong, light, and easy to mould. Some new cars have bumpers made from extra light and strong nanocomposites – plastics mixed with enhancing substances.

Titanium A strong, light aerospace metal similar to aluminium, titanium is used to reduce weight in cars like the Chevrolet Corvette, which has its exhaust made from the metal. Although not rare, titanium costs a lot to process and is much more expensive than aluminium, which tends to be used instead.

When people say cars are **"lumps of metal"**, they're wrong on both counts. A modern car is built with the same attention to detail as a **jet plane** or a **space rocket** – from literally dozens of different materials that are chosen to make the car operate as efficiently as possible.

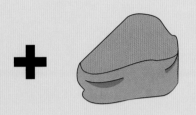

+ 82.5% rock

Iron ore creates the steel for a car's bodywork, engine, and wheels. Sand is used to make glass.

+ 12% oil

Oil is used to produce the plastics found in a car's interior and some engine components.

= 100% car

Leather Car seats evolved from leather horse saddles, which is why luxury cars still have leather interiors today. Plastic is more common in cheaper models. Car makers have tried other materials too – the 1965 Mercer-Cobra had a copper-lined interior.

Laminates Car windscreens are made of a laminate "sandwich" composed from two sheets of glass on the outside with a plastic layer in between. If a stone breaks the outer glass, the impact spreads outwards, and the screen smashes into tiny nuggets. These are less dangerous than larger, sharper pieces.

Platinum

The catalytic converter is the pollution filter in a car's exhaust pipe. It is made from a ceramic honeycomb coated with precious metals such as platinum, which costs about £25,000 per kilogram (£11,000 per pound). Gram for gram, the metal in the catalytic converter is the most expensive material in a car. If the whole vehicle was made from platinum, it would cost over £50,000,000!

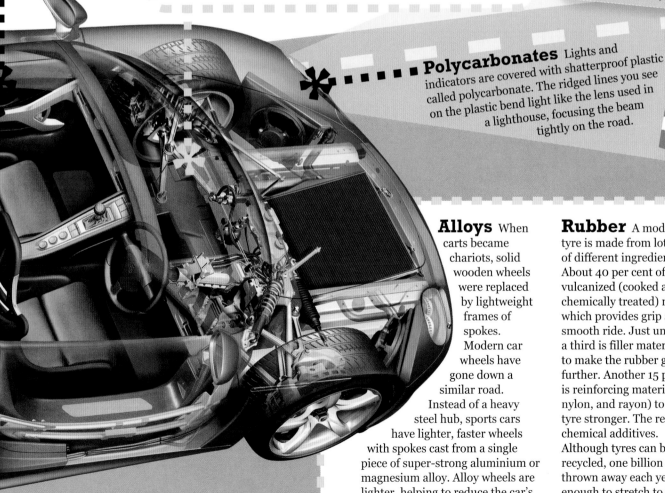

Polycarbonates Lights and indicators are covered with shatterproof plastic called polycarbonate. The ridged lines you see on the plastic bend light like the lens used in a lighthouse, focusing the beam tightly on the road.

Alloys When carts became chariots, solid wooden wheels were replaced by lightweight frames of spokes. Modern car wheels have gone down a similar road. Instead of a heavy steel hub, sports cars have lighter, faster wheels with spokes cast from a single piece of super-strong aluminium or magnesium alloy. Alloy wheels are lighter, helping to reduce the car's weight and improve its handling.

Rubber A modern tyre is made from lots of different ingredients. About 40 per cent of it is vulcanized (cooked and chemically treated) rubber, which provides grip and a smooth ride. Just under a third is filler material to make the rubber go further. Another 15 per cent is reinforcing materials (steel, nylon, and rayon) to make the tyre stronger. The rest is chemical additives. Although tyres can be recycled, one billion are thrown away each year – enough to stretch to the Moon and back.

Electric dreams

There's no engine in an electric car such as the Tesla Roadster. Instead, an electric motor drives the wheels. This set-up has big advantages:

✔ The motor provides 100% torque whatever the revs, providing supercar acceleration.

✔ There's no need for fuel – just plug in to recharge.

✔ Electric cars are cheap to run. The Tesla does the equivalent to 135 miles (217 km) per gallon.

✔ No exhaust fumes or emissions.

✔ Because the powertrain has only a handful of moving parts, the car needs almost no maintenance.

Zap! Electric cars are on the way, with unbelievable acceleration, 100% torque, near-silent motors, and no exhaust – let alone emissions. Could these supercars save the planet? Or is there a catch?

The Tesla Roadster is no battery-powered toy. It may be powered by laptop batteries (6831 of them, to be precise) but its electric motor can accelerate the car from 0 to 60 mph (97 km/h) in 4 seconds and take it to a top speed of 125 mph – yet it barely makes a sound. In fact electric cars are so quiet that artificial *vroom* sounds have to be added so people can hear them coming.

The main drawback with electric cars is the batteries. The Tesla's lithium-ion battery pack weighs nearly half a tonne but can only store as much energy as about 8 litres (1.8 gallons) of petrol. That's still enough to take you 220 miles (354 km), but then you have to stop and re-charge. Which takes 3½ hours. And although the car does not *directly* pollute the air with CO_2 or other emissions, the power station that supplied the electricity may well have used fossil fuels.

Coming soon...

Whizz-wheels

Tomorrow's electric cars could do away with the engine compartment altogether. This ELIICA (ELectric LIthium-Ion Car) has a tiny battery-powered electric motor built into each wheel hub. Eight hub motors give eight times the power and a top speed of over

Wheelie far

Electric cars probably make you think of milk floats that conk out when the batteries go flat. This sporty Mitsubishi hub-motor car couldn't be more different. It can do 124 miles (200 km) on a single charge and has a top speed of 80 mph (130 km/h). It even has solar panels on the roof.

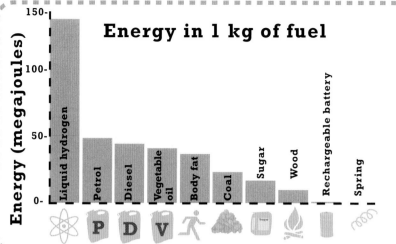

Energy in 1 kg of fuel

Energy (megajoules) — 150, 100, 50, 0

Liquid hydrogen · Petrol · Diesel · Vegetable oil · Body fat · Coal · Sugar · Wood · Rechargeable battery · Spring

P D V

Energy density

The real reason for the amazing success of cars powered by internal combustion is this: petrol and diesel are fantastic at storing energy. A kilogram of petrol or diesel holds far more energy than almost any other kind of fuel you care to mention, except liquid hydrogen or uranium. In other words, petrol and diesel have high "energy density". By contrast, even the best rechargable batteries have very poor energy density, though they will probably improve in the future.

The Hybrid

Short battery range? Then why not carry your own tiny power station on board so you can charge up the batteries on the go. That's the idea behind hybrid cars. They combine the clean pulling power of an electric motor with the long range of a petrol engine. The engine and motor are both capable of driving the wheels, and the car mixes and matches to keep the engine running efficiently. Hybrids and electric cars also use a cunning idea called regenerative braking – when the car brakes, the energy of the wheels is used to generate electricity. Otherwise the energy would simply just be wasted as heat in the brakes.

1 Battery
Think of it as a second fuel tank that supplies electricity to the motors, but one you can top up on the move.

2 Small petrol engine
This drives the wheels and spins the generator. The engine revs at a fairly constant speed, which cuts fuel use.

4 Electric motor
The motor can drive the wheels too. Unlike a petrol engine, it delivers full power and maximum torque from standstill.

3 Generator
This makes electricity to charge the batteries.

A new development is the *tribrid* car – a hybrid with a third, environmentally friendly power source, such as solar power or even a sail.

KEY ▢ Electric motor in use throughout ▨ Petrol engine in use ▢ Battery power in use ▨ Battery recharging

Starting **Normal driving** **Acceleration** **Deceleration** **Stopping and starting**

Engine and motor power are seamlessly combined to fit the driving conditions.

Fully charged

One way to make electric cars go further is to make them lighter. Nissan's Hypermini has plastic panels bolted to a super-light aluminium frame so it uses a quarter as much energy as an ordinary petrol car. Just like a mobile phone, you can plug it in and charge it anywhere.

Sea change

Electricity and water don't mix – unless you're driving a Chinese Tang Hua electric car, that is. Some of these funky yellow bubble cars have electric propellers on the back so you can chug through water. If global warming makes sea levels rise, perhaps we'll all be driving round in these?

Fuel-cell cars

Some car-makers are putting a lot of time and effort into developing hybrid cars where the electric motors are powered by **fuel cells**. The magical fuel that makes this the cleanest, lightest, and most reliable power source yet is **hydrogen.**

The LIFEcar designed by the Morgan Motor Company is powered by eco-friendly fuel-cell technology. It emits nothing more harmful than water.

A fuel cell is a type of battery. Inside it converts the chemicals hydrogen and oxygen into water, and in the process produces electricity. Hydrogen is pumped into the cell from an on-board tank, while the oxygen is taken from the air outside. Together they form steam, which is emitted through the car's exhaust. Remember:

$$2H_2 + O_2 = 2H_2O + ENERGY$$

Many fuel cells are stacked together in layers to increase the amount of electricity produced. This electricity is then stored or sent directly to electric motors that turn the wheels.

The future

Honda FCX Clarity
Honda has become one of the first car manufacturers to produce a family-sized fuel-cell car available for use on the roads. Customers can only lease the car for three years but the FCX Clarity can travel 270 miles (435 km) before needing to refuel.

Microcab
On the streets of Birmingham in England, Microcabs are being used as taxis for short trips. Operated by a scooter-like handlebar and levers, these ultra-light fuel-cell cars have a maximum speed of 30 mph (45 km/h) and need refuelling after 100 miles (160 km).

Fiery fuel

Hydrogen is the most abundant element in the Universe, but it is highly flammable (bursts into flame easily) and, as the lightest gas, it just floats away. However, it can be extracted from water, fossil fuels, and other substances. The tricky thing is to compress (squeeze) it into a tank small enough to fit a car. The tank can be topped up with hydrogen at refuelling stations, but there are very, very few of these at the moment.

The pros and cons

In theory, electric fuel-cell cars could be the answer for clean cars of the future:

✔ Fuel cells are reliable and make little noise as they have no moving parts.

✔ Water is the only thing emitted through the exhaust.

BUT there are a number of challenges still to be overcome:

✘ Increasing the amount of electricity produced so the car has more power.

✘ Compressing and safely storing enough hydrogen into a small tank for hundreds of miles of driving.

✘ Making affordable cars. At the moment, a fuel cell system costs ten times as much to make as a conventional engine.

Electricity is stored in a bank of capacitors.

The fuel tank stores hydrogen. An extremely tough carbon-fibre casing is essential as hydrogen is highly explosive.

Suzuki Sharing Coach

Forget walking – Suzuki have designed a new concept: a single-seater, weatherproof electric pod called a Pixy for roaming the streets. Two Pixys can dock inside a fuel-cell coach, which is used for faster and longer trips while recharging the pods.

Honda Puyo

Imagine being in a car that feels like jelly. The fuel-cell Puyo has a squashable body and silky interior. Fixed to tiny wheels, the cabin can rotate 360 degrees so the car never has to go into reverse.

Design for LIFE

Creating a new car from scratch takes a heck of a lot of hard work, passion, and inspiration, and the hydrogen-powered **Morgan LIFECar** was no exception. It took nearly three years to develop from initial idea to construction of a "prototype" (test car). The ground-breaking car was finally revealed to the world in 2008. Here's how it was made.

1 **The process begins** with hand-drawn sketches. The goal is to create a sporty car that looks classic yet futuristic with great aerodynamics.

2 **A highly detailed** computer model is then made, with every part included.

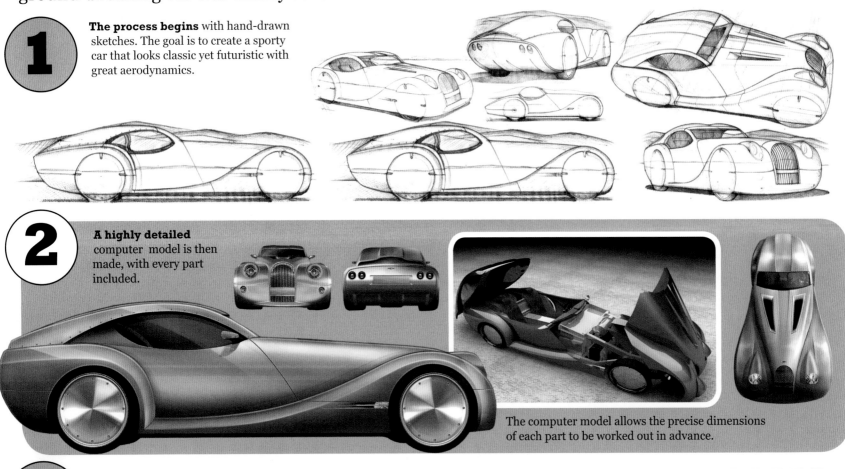

The computer model allows the precise dimensions of each part to be worked out in advance.

3 **The chassis** is created using the measurements from the computer model.

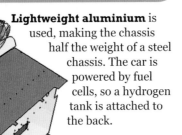

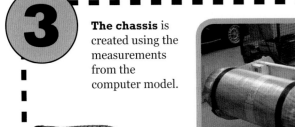

Lightweight aluminium is used, making the chassis half the weight of a steel chassis. The car is powered by fuel cells, so a hydrogen tank is attached to the back.

The electric system is installed. All the driver's controls work electronically – quite unlike most road cars – and a central computer acts as the car's brain.

Engineers check the electronics are working properly by connecting the chassis to a testing machine called a dynamometer.

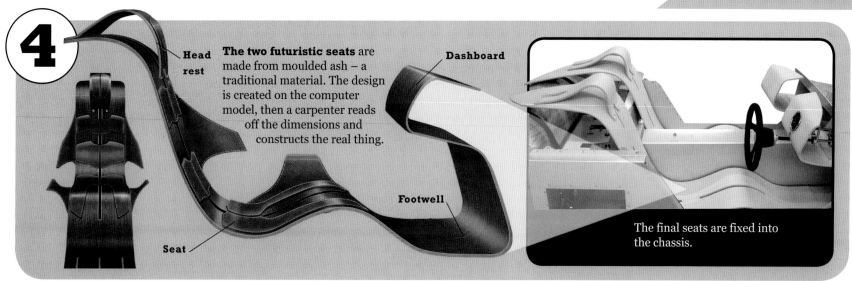

4 The two futuristic seats are made from moulded ash – a traditional material. The design is created on the computer model, then a carpenter reads off the dimensions and constructs the real thing.

Head rest

Dashboard

Seat

Footwell

The final seats are fixed into the chassis.

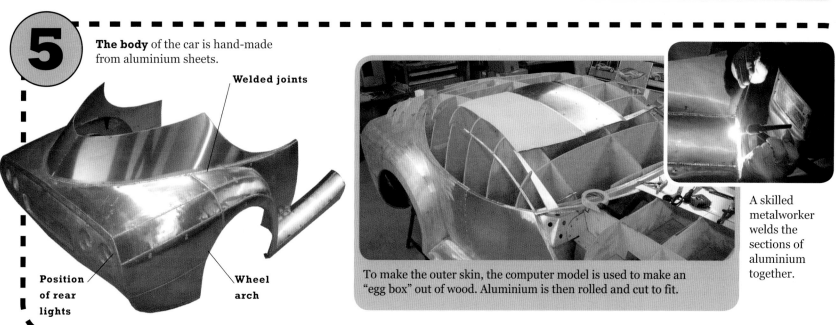

5 The body of the car is hand-made from aluminium sheets.

Welded joints

Position of rear lights

Wheel arch

To make the outer skin, the computer model is used to make an "egg box" out of wood. Aluminium is then rolled and cut to fit.

A skilled metalworker welds the sections of aluminium together.

6 Finally, the chassis and the body are fitted together to make the finished test car, which looks exactly like the computer model. The car is tested for many hours on a track before being taken on the open road for further performance tests.

The LIFEcar is unveiled to the motoring world at the Geneva Motor Show in 2008.

The LIFECar does **0-60** mph (0-96 km/h) in 7 seconds, and energy efficiency is equivalent to 150 miles (241 km) per gallon. And there are **zero emissions**.

Super scuba

An air-filled cabin would make the car too buoyant, so the car is roofless and passengers breathe through scuba gear.

Cabin materials are salt resistant to prevent damage by sea water.

Rear jets blast water backwards to create the force of **THRUST.**

THRUST

To submerge the car, the door is opened so that the cabin floods.

Front jets blast water down to create the force of **LIFT.**

LIFT

THRUST

Inspired by James Bond's submersible Lotus Esprit in the film *The Spy Who Loved Me*, the Rinspeed sQuba is the world's first and only fully submersible car. It can drive on land (top speed 75 mph or 120 km/h), ride on water like a boat, or submerge completely to become a submarine. Propulsion comes from a set of water jets that blast water both down and backwards; Newton's third law supplies the resulting forces of **THRUST** and **LIFT** that make the car "swim". Agent 007 would doubtless admire the updated look of the Lotus Elise on which the sQuba is based, but he might not be so impressed with its top speed under water: a mere 1.9 mph (3 km/h). Which is a lot less than walking speed.

Crikey! They're lost!

*

The body is based on the Lotus Elise sports car.

1 Sky car
Avoid the traffic, commute by UFO! This flying saucer from the 1960s could take off and land vertically. A set of fans encircling the two (terrified) passengers blasted air earthwards; Newton's third law provided the equal and opposite force needed to lift the saucer. Loads of fun, but commercially speaking it never got off the ground. And it didn't actually work.

TOP 10 mad ideas

There's a fine line between genius and madness. Here are some of the wildest car ideas that scientists and inventors have come up with in the last 100 years.

2 Jeep Hurricane
Why steer a car with just the front wheels? This tough off-roader can steer each wheel independently, enabling it to drive diagonally or spin round on the spot by running two wheels forwards and two backwards. There are two engines: one at the front (wherever that is) and one at the back.

3 Pivo 2
This bubbly little three-seat, electric concept car has a cabin that can rotate to face any direction. Handy for those sharp bends? Not really, it can only rotate when the car has parked. It also boasts a robot driving companion, who judges the driver's mood from their facial expressions and tone of voice, and chats to keep them cheerful. It looks like the future of back-seat drivers is in safe hands – of robots.

Beam me up Scotty!

4 Covini C6W

Why do most cars have only four wheels? This 185 mph (300 km/h) supercar has six, with the front four used to steer. Extra wheels give a smooth and safer ride. With more rubber in contact with the road, the Covini has extra grip – wheelie more friction! The front four are smaller that the rear two, making the car more aerodynamic. So is six better than four? Well, a six-wheeled F1 car won the Swedish Grand Prix in 1976. I'll let you make up your own minds.

Rinspeed Presto

Why are parking spaces always too small? They aren't with this Swiss concept car – at the touch of a button it goes from a four to a two-seat roadster, shortening by 0.75 m (2.5 ft). It's the "incredible shrinking car". The designers had to make sure the chassis remained strong whatever its length. If they hadn't it would have been the "incredible bendy car", as the chassis would flex while driving and lead to dangerous handling.

5

It's important your back-seat passengers get out first.

Electric motors pull front and back together. Nice and snug!

6 Purves Dynasphere

Why have the hassle of a car body and four wheels, when you can have a human-sized hamster wheel. Looks like fun? Not really – it had a top speed of only 25 mph (40 km/h) and was impossible to steer. Not its only problem, as stopping was also a tricky manoeuvre – momentum dictates that under sudden braking the seat would go round with the wheel. Still, just think of all those car washing chores you'd get out of.

7 Leyat Helica

What happened to the wings? This 1920s French car avoided the complexity of the engine driving the wheels by putting a 1.4 m (4.5 ft) propeller on the front to push air backwards and so pull the car forwards, just like an aeroplane. Not as silly as it sounds, as it reached speeds of over 100 mph (160 km/h). Fast, light, and aerodynamic, though not strong on pedestrian safety.

8 Ford Nucleon

In the 1950s nuclear power was the future! In this never-built car, a hot radioactive core would convert water into steam to spin turbines, which drove the wheels and generated electricity. Cores would need swapping at special nuclear refuelling stations every 5000 miles (8000 km). Economic yes, but would you like driving around with a radioactive core under the bonnet? Car crashes could have been very messy!

9 Hannomag

A basket-case of an idea. Innovative 1920s German designers built this car's body from wicker – woven plant stalks – a giant, driveable dog basket. Cheap, but strong compared with its weight, it was the carbon fibre of its day. Unfortunately, construction was very fiddly and when the car got wet it had a tendency to rot. That pesky rain!

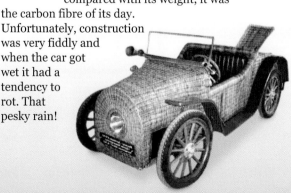

10 Mazda Taiki

This super-spacey sports car of the future channels air over its sleek body, creating as little disturbance as possible. This keeps energy-wasting drag to an absolute minimum and saves fuel. Thin tyres reduce friction with the road and an ultra-efficient "rotary engine" gives loads of acceleration, and keeps the exhaust fumes lung-friendly. Who said green cars had to be boring?

Monster trucks are essentially a pickup truck body mounted on a bus axle connected to enormous wheels. With their sophisticated suspension systems they can bounce over almost anything.

Glossary

ABS
Anti-lock brake system. An electronic control system that applies a car's brakes in short bursts to prevent skidding.

acceleration
A change in velocity. Acceleration happens when things speed up, slow down, or move in a different direction.

aerodynamics
The science of designing smoothly shaped cars and other vehicles so they travel faster and waste less energy as they move through the air.

airflow
The pattern of air movement around a moving vehicle. Airflow is invisible, unless studied under special conditions in a wind tunnel.

alloy
An alloy is a mixture of a metal with smaller quantities of other metals (and sometimes non-metals) to make it harder, able to survive high temperatures, or improve it in other ways. Alloy wheels use strong, lightweight alloys based on aluminium.

axle
A sturdy metal rod on which the wheels of a car rotate.

battery
Device that generates electric power through chemical reactions.

biofuel
A type of fuel, made without using petroleum, that can be used in an ordinary internal combustion engine. Biofuels can be produced from such things as sugar cane and vegetable oil.

brake
A mechanical device that stops a car by converting its kinetic energy into heat. Most cars use disc brakes, which press synthetic fibres against discs inside the wheels to slow them.

centripetal force
Cars need help to go around a corner. Objects tend to travel in straight lines unless centripetal force bends their motion round into a curve.

centre of gravity
The point where the weight of an object appears to be concentrated, usually near its middle. Cars with a high centre of gravity are more likely to topple over when they go round corners.

combustion
The process of burning a fuel with oxygen from the air to release energy, producing steam and carbon dioxide as by-products. Unless things burn completely, toxic exhaust gases such as carbon monoxide and other forms of pollution are also produced.

crankshaft
A rotating axle that carries power from the pistons in an engine to the gearbox.

cylinder
A strong metal canister inside a car's engine where fuel is burned to produce heat energy. Most cars have between 2 and 12 cylinders.

Combustion chamber

Diesel engine
A type of engine that compresses the air before the fuel is injected so that it ignites without the need for a spark plug. Diesel engines burn heavier oil than petrol, and are more efficient than petrol engines. They produce high torque at relatively low speeds, ideal for trucks and buses.

Steering system

differential
Pumpkin-shaped gearbox that allows the wheels on opposite sides of a car to turn at different speeds when going round a corner.

downforce
The force that pushes down on an aerodynamically shaped vehicle, such as a Formula One car, when air moves rapidly over it. Downforce is the opposite of lift (the force that makes an aeroplane take off as it moves quickly forward through the air).

drag
The force of air resistance that slows a car as it moves faster. At high speeds, virtually all a car's power is used to overcome drag.

efficiency
The fraction of the energy that a machine uses effectively compared with how much is put in. A typical petrol engine is 30 per cent efficient, so it uses 30 per cent of the energy in the petrol to move the car forwards and wastes the other 70 per cent, mostly as heat.

elasticity
The tendency of a material to return to its original shape if a force is applied and then removed. A car's rubber tyres are elastic, so they spring back to shape after running over bumps in the road.

electric motor
A machine that uses electricity and magnetism to power an axle. An electric motor converts electrical energy into mechanical energy.

energy
A property of matter that has the ability to make something happen through movement or a change in condition. These changes can be physical or chemical, and allow energy to be converted to another form. For example, the chemical energy of fuel is converted into heat and then into mechanical energy in an engine.

force
See next page

friction
The rubbing force between two surfaces that come into contact. Friction between the tyres of a car and the road beneath tends to slow it down, as does the friction between air moving around a car and the metal bodywork.

fuel
A substance that can be burned in air to release energy. Fuels such as petrol are made mostly of hydrocarbons (molecules made from carbon and hydrogen).

fuel cell
An electrical device powered by fuel from a tank that makes electricity through a chemical reaction. A fuel cell is similar to a large battery, but where a battery gradually runs down, a fuel cell runs continuously for as long as there is fuel in the tank.

gear
A wheel with teeth cut into its edge that meshes with one or more similar wheels to increase the speed or torque of an engine. The gearbox in a car contains gear wheels of different sizes that mesh together to make the car go faster, increase its climbing power up hills, or drive in reverse.

Gears

gravity
The pulling force (force of attraction) between any two masses in the Universe. On Earth, we experience gravity as a downward force that makes things fall towards the ground.

heat
A form of energy consisting of atoms and molecules moving about randomly.

horsepower
A measurement of the amount of power a car engine can produce. In metric units, 1 horsepower = 746 watts – roughly the power produced by twelve 60-watt lightbulbs.

hybrid car
Hybrid cars have two sources of power: an ordinary petrol engine, powered by a fuel tank, and an electric motor, powered by batteries. The car can switch between petrol and electric power to suit different conditions.

hydraulics
A hydraulic system can transmit force between two places by pushing fluids through tubes of different sizes. Hydraulic pipes power the brakes on most cars. They also power the lifting rams on bulldozers and cranes.

hydrogen
A light, invisible, and highly flammable gas that can be used to make power in a fuel cell.

inertia
The tendency of an object to stay still or move with a steady speed until a force acts on it.

internal combustion engine
An engine that burns fuel inside closed metal cylinders. External combustion engines, such as steam engines, produce power less efficiently by burning fuel in an external chamber to heat a liquid or gas, which then moves a piston or a turbine.

jet engine
An engine that makes power by burning a continuous stream of fuel and air. A jet engine moves a plane or car forwards by firing a stream of hot gas backwards – a scientific idea known as action and reaction (or Newton's third law).

kinetic energy
When something moves it is said to have kinetic energy. To make a moving car stop, all its kinetic energy must be converted into other forms (by heating up the brakes, for example).

Pistons

machine
In science, any device that transmits or modifies power, forces, or motion to do work can be classed as a machine. A spanner, a jack, and a crowbar, used for changing tyres are all "simple machines".

mechanical
Describes any device that works using moving parts (unlike an electrical or electronic device, which may have no moving parts).

mass
The amount of matter something contains, measured in grams, kilograms, or tonnes.

momentum
The tendency of a moving object to keep moving. The momentum of an object is its mass times its velocity, so trucks generally have more momentum than cars, and fast-moving cars have more momentum than slower ones.

piston
A tight-fitting plunger that moves up and down inside an engine cylinder, pushed by the force of exploding fuel. The pistons power the crankshaft. Energy from the pistons drives the gearbox and ultimately the wheels. Also used in shock absorbers to convert the energy of bouncing suspension springs into heat.

Differential

pollution
A harmful or otherwise unwanted chemical created when engines burn fuel. Exhaust pollution is a mixture of gases (such as carbon monoxide) and solids (including soot).

Force
A pushing or pulling action that can make objects speed up or slow down, change direction, or change shape.

PUSH

potential energy
Most physical systems contain stored, or potential, energy that can be turned into other kinds of useful energy at a later time. A car at the top of a hill has potential energy because of its position. It can turn its potential energy into kinetic energy by rolling down the slope.

pressure
The force exerted by something pressing or squeezing an area. The tyres on a car are under pressure because air, forced into them, pushes against their rubber walls.

rocket engine
A jet engine that carries its own supply of oxygen rather than taking in oxygen from the air.

rpm
Revolutions ("revs") per minute. The number of times a wheel rotates in one minute.

shock absorber
A piston that moves in a cylinder filled with oil or gas that can absorbs the bumps in a road. Shock absorbers are part of a car's suspension system.

SPEED
A measurement of how fast a car is going. You can work out a car's speed by dividing the distance it travels by the time it takes.

steam engine
An engine fueled by coal or oil that heats water to make steam. The steam pushes pistons back and forth to drive one or more wheels.

streamlining
The smooth, usually curved shape of a vehicle designed to reduce drag and improve performance.

Tyre

Crash test dummies go through accidents day after day without complaint. The black and yellow markings act as reference points for calculating the distances and speeds at which the dummy travels during collisions.

suspension
A series of components attached to the wheels of a car to make the ride feel smoother for passengers by reducing the effects of vertical motion as the wheels go over bumps. The suspension includes tyres, springs, and shock absorbers.

torque
Measure of turning force about an axis. Car engines with high torque can produce a great deal of force to make the car go quickly.

tread
Ridged patterns in car tyres that help to increase friction and grip on the road.

turbulence
The disrupted air pattern produced by a car body that is not properly streamlined. The more turbulence a car produces, the harder it has to work to move through the air, the slower it goes, and the more energy it wastes.

velocity
Velocity is the rate at which a moving car changes its position when travelling in a given direction. If a car goes around a corner without changing speed, its velocity changes because it changes direction.

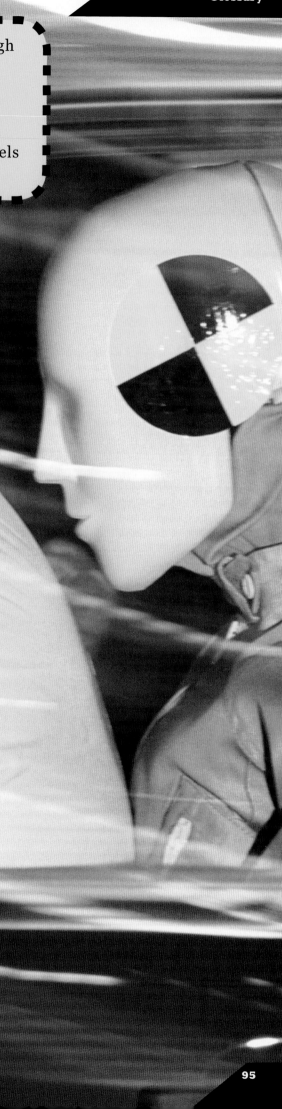

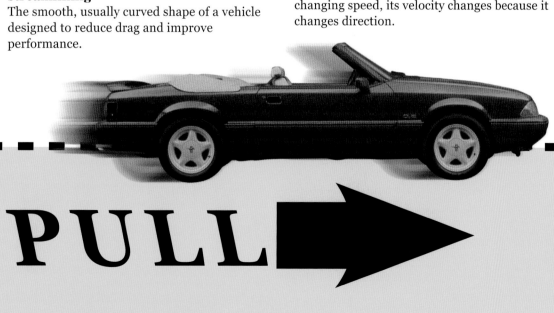

PULL →

Index

Acknowledgements

Dorling Kindersley would like to thank Sonia Moore, Jess Bentall, Joanna Pocock, and Gemma Fletcher for design assistance; and Cécile Landau and Carrie Love for editorial help.

The publisher would also like to thank the following for their kind permission to reproduce their photographs: (Key: a-above; b-below/bottom; c-centre; f-far; l-left; r-right; t-top)

Alamy Images: Aflo Foto Agency 43tr; Sally Ann Baines 72l; Joe Baraban 3bc, 20-21; Simon Batley 33br; blickwinkel 49clb; Steve Bloom Images 41l; Clark Brennan 62-63t; T. Bucket 2cla (green car); Caro 59r; John Crall 49crb; CrashPA 69bl, 69cl, 69tl; Drive Images 23cl, 41crb; Drive Images / eVox 11cb; ICP 45br, 45ca, 45ca (layer1), 45ca (layer2), 45ca (layer3), 45ca (layer4), 45cr, 45crb; izmostock 44crb; John James 84br; John Lamm 49tl; Lemonlight Features 16crb; Mary Evans Picture Library 91cr; Iain Masterton 2-3br, 91br; Motoring Picture Library 3ca (Black car), 16, 25cl, 41c, 41clb, 44cr, 49tr; Thomas Müller 73bl; National Motor Museum / Motoring Picture Library 2-3cra (Thrust), 53bl; NewSports 92; Edward Parker 59c; Paolo Patrizi 2bl, 85br; pbpgalleries 3cla (flying car); 91cl; Picturesbyrob / Tf3 3ca (knocked back), 42-43, 75cl; Steven Poe 3cra (tyre), 58bc; Friedrich Saurer 77cra, 77tl; Mark Scheuern 72br, 80bl, 90; James Schwabel 42, 51tc; Guy Spangenberg 56cr; T-Bucket 7tr, 23bl; Wilmar Topshots 34; Transtock Inc. / Glenn Paulina 33tr; Jim West 11crb, 83br, 85tc; **Ariel Motor Company:** 3cla (below thermal car), 44br, 46-47; **Audi UK** - a trading division of Volkswagen Group United Kingdom Limited: 15tr, 35bl, 97; George Augustine 23br; **Bugatti Automobiles S.A.S.:** 2clb (white interior), 2-3cr, 3cr (knock back), 26-27 (all images); **Candy Lab:** 82; **Chrysler and Jeep Marketing:** 49cl; **Citroën Communication:** 22cr; **Corbis:** Bruce Benedict/Transtock 48c; Bettmann 10cla, 10crb, 11c, 43ftl, 52bc, 52bl, 52br, 52tc, 52tl, 53tl, 58tr, 91crb; Car Culture 2tc, 3clb (Blue car), 23bc, 24bl, 24br, 49cr, 49cra, 73bc, 82br, 84bl, 85bl; Leonard de Selva 32br, 33cr, 53cla; Rick Doyle 16cl; Duomo 2cr (yellow racing car); Ferrari/epa/ 68tr; Noboru Hashimoto 3cra (small purple car), 90br; Bob Krist 22cl; Matthias Kulka / Zefa 17bc, 30ftr; Lavandeira Jr / Epa 31 (ship); David Madison 75bl; Museum of Flight 5bl, 78-79; Frederic Pitchal 77br; Reuters 83bl; Kim Sayer 25cr; Schlegelmilch 2bl (red racing car); 7b, 21cr, 23cr, 49br, 50-51, 65br, 66b, 66t, 67b, 67t, 68c; Wolfram Schroll/zefa 57br; Ted Soqui 74c; Hans Strand 31 (road); George Tiedemann 11br; Yuriko Nakao/Reuters 82bl; **Covini Engineering:** 91tl; **DK Images:** Design Museum, London 18br; Kit Houghton 18tl, 19c, 40cra; Dave King 24cr, 45crb (dog), 45crb (rabbit), 45tr; Museum of the Regiments, Calgary Regiments, Calgary 19bc (r); Museum of Transportation, St Louis, Missouri 31 (train); National Motor Museum, Beaulieu 3tc, 59bc, 59bl ((a)), 59bl ((b)), 59bl ((c)), 59br ((a)), 59br ((b)), 59br ((c)); Stephen Oliver 44t; Toro Wheelhorse UK Ltd 19bl; Toro Wheelhorse UK Ltd 24cl; Matthew Ward 77cra (car); **Getty Images:** John William Banagan 4bl; The Bridgeman Art Library / Sir Godfrey Kneller 64clb; Timothy Clary/AFP 69clb; Guy Edwardes 40cb; Hola Images 29ftr; Holloway 40bc, 41cb; Zena Holloway 48; Keystone / Hulton Archive 53tr; Stone / John William Banagan 38-39; Taxi / Miguel S Salmeron 2clb (rear of red car pulling away); Nick Veasey 68bl; Michael Wildsmith 44bl; Konrad Wothe 40crb; **© GM Corp.:** 2tr, 3cb; **Honda** (UK): 42cra; **Hummer:** 60-61; **Lamborghini:** 48b; **Mazda Simon Europe GmbH:** 3crb, 15tl, 25br, 25crb (Rotary engine); **Mercedes-Benz:** 48clb; courtesy the Michelin Tyre Public Limited Company: 59cla, 59clb; **Photo provided by Moller International, USA.:** 90t; Morgan Motor Company Ltd: 3tr, 84-85c, 86-87; **Motoring Picture Library/ national Motor Museum:** 52tr; **North American Eagle, Inc.:** 52-53; **PA Photos:** 2br; AP Photo / Xinhua, Fang Xi 2crb, 54-55; AP Photo/Xinhua, Fang Xi 5tl; Tim Ockenden 2clb (black supersonic car), 41bl, 41cr; **Photolibrary:** Ted Kinsman 2tl, 12cl, 13cr; **Porsche AG:** 80-81; **PunchStock:** Corbis 73tl; **Reuters:** 70-71; **Rinspeed Inc.:** 3br, 6bl, 88-89, 91tr; **Dieter J. Schaefer:** 4tl, 8-9; **Rex Schneider:** 2cl (basket car); **Science & Society Picture Library:** Science Museum 10ca, 11clb; **Science Photo Library:** 69cr; Cody Images 3clb (Man); Dr Jeremy Burgess 56tl; Gustoimages 69tr; Ton Kinsbergen 56cl; Ted Kinsman 3tl, 56br; Laguna Design 12crb, 13clb, 30bl, 30tr; Hank Morgan 3bl, 49bl; Paul Rapson 30cla, 30fcla, 57bl; Sheila Terry 18bl; Dr. Arthur Tucker 69br; **Shutterstock:** Michael Stokes 2bc, 62-63; **Sutton Motorsport:** 2cra, 68br, 69c; **Dan Taylor:** 81cl; **TopFoto.co.uk:** 53br; Roger-Viollet 53tc; **Toyota (GB) PLC:** 83; **Wikipedia, The Free Encyclopedia:** 66bl

All other images © Dorling Kindersley
For further information see: **www.dkimages.com**